The Twelfth Night

A Scandinavian Dark Advent novel set in Greenland

~ Petra *Piitalaat* Jensen Book 2 ~

by Christoffer Petersen

And what should I do in Illyria?
My brother he is in Elysium.

— *Twelfth Night, Act I, Sc. II*

William Shakespeare (1564-1616)

Introduction

I remember walking with my wife to the hospital in Uummannaq, one long, dark winter night. It was pitch black. The sea ice was almost thick enough to walk on, and hardy hunters had been sledging to their fishing lines for about a week. Jane was on night shift at the hospital, and I said goodnight to her at the door. As soon as the door closed, I heard a shout and the slap of feet on the ice covering the road. I stopped a few feet from the entrance to the hospital and watched a group of Greenlanders, three men in their twenties, run down the hill from the police station, past the hospital.

They didn't stop.

Then I saw the masked figure chasing them. Its upper body was padded like an upturned triangle, and it was carrying a large stick. Its face bulged and twisted, and there was steam chuffing out of the slit between the carved wooden teeth.

It was January 6th.

It was *mitaartut*.

It was the Twelfth Night.

Chris
December 2018
Denmark

The Twelfth Night

A Scandinavian Dark Advent novel set in Greenland

~ Petra *Piitalaat* Jensen Book 2 ~

Ataasinngorneq

Monday, 5th January 2043
Nuuk, Greenland

Chapter 1

The coloured paste was thin and sticky between her fingers, like blood. Natuk Petersen smoothed it into her hair, working it to the roots. She braced herself against the plastic veneer covering the bulkhead as the captain drove the trawler through the waves at the mouth of Nuuk fjord. They would be at the tourist dock within twenty minutes. Natuk worked more paste into her hair, turning and dipping her head to see as much of it as possible in the greasy mirror, cracked and scabbed at the edges with rust. Gone were the shiny black locks that turned people's heads on the street, replaced with a rough-hewn bob of blonde that seemed to repel her coffee-cream skin. Natuk washed her fingers and rinsed her hair. She left her thick eyebrows black.

There was a bump, and the slow scrape of the metal hull along the thick sea-greened wood of the dock. Natuk dressed, anticipating the knock on the door as she pulled a thick woollen sweater over her head, tucked the FNS-40 compact pistol into the back of her jeans and buttoned the fly.

"See you on deck," she called out at the quick rap of knuckles on the bathroom door.

There was a twist of magic in the early morning darkness pressing the wooden houses, the high rises, and the commercial and industrial units of Nuuk into the granite. The very weight of the darkness, the dense cold – it could almost be seen bearing down on old eaves, arches and roofs, mocking the newer buildings. Natuk tugged on her retro brown duvet jacket as she climbed onto the deck, studying the horizon as she lifted her foot and pressed it onto the railings to tie her laces. She could just see the lights of Little Amsterdam in the distance, sparkling above the city of Nuuk. Beyond that, a little to the south, she imagined the dragon tails and lanterns of Chinatown, and then the bridge across the fjord to the American Coast Guard base – out of sight and out of bounds.

"We'll see about that," she said.

Natuk adjusted the grip of the pistol pressing into the small of her back, nodded at the man waiting by the gangplank onto the dock and followed him off the trawler.

The lights of Little Amsterdam were lost as Natuk walked behind the tall Greenlander, Angut Samuelsen, her protection for the evening. He wore a pair of thick glasses, and Natuk caught the flicker of his eyes as Angut scanned the local security data streaming onto the lens. Natuk's brother had streamed his own death with a similar pair of glasses just two weeks earlier. Natuk bit her lip, shook the thought out of her mind, and slipped her own glasses onto her face. The thick black rims complemented her thick black brows, accentuated by the short blonde cut of her hair and the tight set of her jaw. *Tonight isn't about appearances*, she thought, as she logged into the same DataStream as Angut, flicking her eyes through the options on the navigation screen and selecting the shortest and least populated route to the first location on a short list of two.

Angut stopped at the bottom of a long set of concrete steps leading to the road. He frowned at the sound of voices and reached for his Beretta APX pistol, heavier and bulkier than Natuk's. She slapped at his hand and shook her head. Pressing him against a streetlamp, her hands on his cheeks and her lips on his mouth as a party of three late-night revellers, stumbled down the steps towards the dock. They cheered as they passed, and Natuk framed a shy smile on her lips until they were gone.

"Keep your pistol in your pants," she said and nodded towards the steps.

She followed Angut to the top, checked their route, and blinked to trigger the *confirm* command on the lens view screen. A pulse of music turned her head, and another blink on the map projected onto the lens confirmed that the beat came from the second and final location on the list. She centred the map with another blink, tucked her hands inside the voluminous pockets of her jacket, crunching the snow beneath the thick tread of her boots as she picked up the pace. Angut followed, a single pace behind her as they walked deeper into Nuuk, passing the outlying buildings, their faces glowing with neon reds and greens, the Christmas stars shining on their glasses from the windows, and the litter of the holidays drifting past their heels as a thin wind spindrifted down Nuuk's main pedestrianised street.

The vacant store with metal plates bolted over the windows, and burn marks scoring the edges, was at the end of the street, on the left, within spitting distance of Greenland's National Library. Natuk waited for another clump of Greenlanders enjoying the prolonged Christmas and Independence celebrations to weave past them, smiling coyly as she slipped her arm around Angut, dragging him away from the more amorous of the group.

"He's mine," she said, when a woman reached for him, spilling her drink on the snow.

"There's more than enough to share," the woman

said.

Natuk gave the woman a lingering glance. "Maybe later," she said, smiling at the jeers and cat-calling as they moved on. She pulled Angut into the scarred entrance to the store as soon as they were gone and knocked on the door. It creaked open a second later, a hand's width, the length of the thick security chain. A small nut-brown hand pressed a retinal scanner through the gap. Natuk removed her glasses and slipped them inside her jacket. She pressed her eye to the screen and waited for the man to unchain the door and let them in.

The man turned on the lights as soon as the door was closed, revealing a sterile surface of thick clear plastic covering the burned walls and floor. Three rows of plastic tables dominated the centre of the room, with more tables pressed against the walls. Slim screens and computers plugged into suitcase-like battery packs glowed from the wall tables, casting a soft light onto the centre tables covered in drone parts and spares spilling onto the surfaces.

"You realise these have to be ready by morning?" Natuk said.

"*Aap.*"

"Will they be?"

The man scratched at the thin stubble on his cheek and nodded. "I have more people helping me."

"Where are they?"

"Out back." He frowned. "I didn't think you wanted them to see you."

"Whatever." Natuk shrugged.

"Keep them there," Angut said. He reached for a packet of propellers on the table. "What about the cold?"

"They are polar oiled, and the batteries are Arctic-grade," the man said. "They'll work."

"And you'll sync them with the glasses?" Natuk asked, pointing at the banks of computers along the wall.

"We're syncing them as we build them. You'll have full control."

"Then we're done," she said.

Natuk walked to the door, waited for Angut to join her, and then stepped outside. She heard the chain snick into place a second after the man shut the door behind them.

"This was one of the buildings Ooqi paid someone to torch before Christmas," Natuk said.

The thought of her brother, and his campaign to spoil the referendum for Greenlandic independence chilled her more than the cold pressing down from the winter sky. She considered the difference in their approaches, how his had been the spectacular campaign of terror, making dramatic use of dead bodies. Natuk smiled as they walked to the second location, following Angut's lead via the map on his view screen. Her campaign was a last-ditch effort designed to sour all thoughts of independence and play on the young and their distrust of the older corrupt ministers in government. It would be more explosive than Ooqi's campaign. It had to be. *Besides*, she thought, *they brought this on themselves. They deserve it – for their ignorance, and for my brother, for he is in Elysium.*

Angut stopped and pointed towards a building across the street. "They're here," he said.

Natuk waited for Angut to gather the small group of young Greenlanders, all of them aged within a year or two of Natuk's twenty-five years. All of them selected because of their dissident attitudes and comments posted across the social media and message boards connecting them across the city, and in the private cyber arena Natuk had created for them. She watched as they pulled spray cans of black paint from their pockets and showed Angut the acetate stencils tucked between the layers of their clothes. He nodded, gave them their instructions, and waited for them to disperse before walking back to Natuk.

"They're ready," he said. "They've cached stencils and paint across the city. They'll post the locations on the forums as soon as they have finished."

"I counted seven," Natuk said. "That's not enough."

Angut grinned. "They were the *team leaders*. There's more waiting."

"Okay."

Angut reached for Natuk's arm, pressing his thick fingers around her bicep as he lowered his glasses.

"What?"

"Are you sure about the next step?" he said. "I don't think you should go alone."

Natuk brushed his hand away and took a step back. "Just meet me at the dock. I'll be back within two hours."

Angut pressed his glasses onto his nose and gestured for Natuk to do the same.

"No," she said. "I'm going offline for a bit."

She tugged the pistol from her jeans and pressed it into Angut's hand, turning her back on him before he could protest. Natuk walked along the street, past the library, tuning into the pulse of music and following it to a heavily-guarded door, allowing herself to be frisked and groped by the Âmo security guards before pushing past the bouncers and kicking the snow from her boots. She walked into the nightclub as the third and last of the guards at the door opened it and nodded for her to go inside.

The music shuddered and phased up the narrow stairs as Natuk squinted into the dark, compensating for the vibrant neon blues and purples blitzing in waves across the walls to the beat, the thud and stutter of the most notorious of Greenland's nightclubs: *Amâgaiat* – the troll that eats lonely travellers. *Or tourists and foreigners*, Natuk thought as she scanned the crowds of dancers. She looked beyond the throng of bodies on the dance floor, stepping onto a raised platform beside the bar to see past the young men and women teasing at each other's hair and slipping their hands over each other's bodies in the booths beyond the dance floor. She could have put on her glasses. She could have run a quick facial scan and located her mark within seconds, but Natuk knew it wasn't necessary. The girl she was looking for would stand out from the crowd – any crowd – always.

"Hey. Staff only."

Natuk glanced at the young man behind the bar as he shooed her away and into the crowd. She turned away, pausing as a twist of three bodies bumped into her. Natuk recovered her balance, lifted her head, and looked right into the eyes of a young woman – Natuk knew she was twenty years old – perched on the edge of a seat at the booth furthest from the dance floor. The girl's eyes softened as she recognised Natuk. She started to rise, but Natuk lifted her hand.

"Stay there," Natuk mouthed, as she slid between

the dancers writhing like snakes on the dance floor, until she reached the steps to the boothed area. Natuk smiled at the young woman as she walked past the booths and reached out with her hand.

"Natuk?" the woman asked.

"*Aap.*"

"I recognised you – your smile – from the photo you sent."

"*All* of them?"

"No," the woman said. She blushed as Natuk tugged at her hand and pulled her to her feet.

"Maybe later," Natuk said with a raised eyebrow, as she guided the woman to an empty table along the wall leading to the toilets.

They sat down, and Natuk pressed her fingers into the woman's hands, squeezing her fingers into a lattice, catching them in a web. The woman's cheeks coloured, her eyes soft in the neon light, her hair long and black, clinging to Natuk's cheeks as they kissed.

Natuk pulled back with a laugh.

The woman frowned, her eyes darting with confused flecks of fear and arousal.

"What is it? What have I done?"

"Done?" Natuk said. "You've haven't *done* anything."

"Then why are you laughing?"

"Because, Tiina Markussen," Natuk said. "I don't think I have ever met anyone so perfect."

"Is that a bad thing?"

"No, Tiina, it's not."

Natuk slipped her hand around Tiina's neck, felt the heat of her skin prickle against her palm, and pulled her close, pressing her lips on Tiina's, teasing her with a single lingering bite, and the promise of so much more.

Chapter 2

The bathroom tiles of the hotel suite warmed the soles of her feet as Pipaluk Uutaaq, Greenland's First Minister, leaned over the bathroom sink to brush her cheeks with a medium blush. She tiptoed for a closer look at her mouth, pressing the lipstick into the creases of her lips as she lightly gripped the edge of the bathroom unit. She heard a man's voice call out from the bedroom and ignored him, focusing instead on her lips, a crisp touch of eyeliner and some shadow. She rested on her feet, enjoying the warmth of the under floor heating, as she fastened her black bra around her stomach, turned it so the clasp was behind her back and slipped the lacy cups over her small breasts. The light around the mirror lit the straps on her dark skin, and she smiled as she brushed her bobbed hair into stylish layers with a sharp cut of the fringe framing her chin. Model-chic with just the right amount of colour for the cameras, set off by a white blouse. She tugged at the silk, lifting the blouse from her bra, wondering if black was too much, deciding that she didn't care.

"Daddy would have been proud of his little girl," she said, assuming a younger voice and a childish tilt of her chin. She altered her voice to a more ministerial pitch. "My father would be so proud of us, our people, our land, on the cusp of freedom from colonial influence, only months away from true independence."

Pipaluk frowned, plucking her tablet from the towel shelf. She highlighted the word *cusp* and searched for an alternative. *Pinnacle* sounded wrong, *zenith* too obscure. She settled on *eve*.

"On the *eve* of our independence."

"Pipaluk? Can I come in?"

"*Naamik*," she said, as she scrolled through her speech.

"I need to pee."

"There's a bathroom down the hall, by the bar."

"Pipaluk?"

She opened the door, glanced at the man's pale skin and handed him a towel.

"You might want to cover yourself up."

Pipaluk closed the door, ignored the man's curse, and reminded herself that the next time her husband was out of town, she would choose an older lover for the weekend, more robust, less Danish. She smiled at the sound of the door closing.

She sat on the toilet to pull on a pair of tights, stood up to fasten her skirt around her waist, and grabbed her tablet on the way out of the bathroom. Pipaluk stuffed the tablet into her briefcase, slipped her feet inside fleece-lined boots and her arms into the thick *Canada Goose* quilted jacket – still Greenland's favourite after all these years. She stopped at the door, remembered her shoes, and tucked them under her arm as she left the suite.

Pipaluk met her weekend lover in the corridor, returning from the toilets by the bar.

"I'll have someone from reception check the room in twenty minutes. Try not to forget anything," she said, as she brushed past him.

"You're a real bitch, First Minister."

Pipaluk stopped. "You think so?"

"I do," the man said. "Lots of people do."

"Yours or mine?"

"What?"

She rolled her eyes. "Danes or Greenlanders?"

"Does it matter?"

"Not anymore," she said, as she turned her back on him. Pipaluk heard him slam the door to the suite as she waited for the elevator. "Like father like daughter," she said, as the doors opened. She caught the reflection of her smile in the polished tiles inside the elevator, pressed the button to go down, and let the smile grow for at least another two floors. By the time she reached the lobby, Greenland's First Minister was all business.

"Your first meeting with the minister for fishing and hunting has been cancelled," her assistant said, as soon as the elevator doors opened.

"Really?"

Juuarsi Fleischer swiped the tablet in his hands. "The minister said he was feeling sick. Although, there are conflicting accounts as to what *kind* of sickness."

"It can wait, Juuarsi," Pipaluk said, as she stopped by the reception desk. "Let him enjoy the celebrations. He's earned it," she said, and smiled at the receptionist. "We all have."

"Yes, First Minister," the receptionist said.

"There's a man in my room. He needs to leave. Will you check for me?"

"Of course." The young woman smiled. "When should I check?"

"Give him ten minutes. No longer." Pipaluk smiled and followed her assistant to the door.

Juuarsi waved for the First Minister's driver to approach the entrance, and then held the door for Pipaluk to get inside the spacious electric SUV. The interior matched her outfit, and she shrugged her jacket off and onto the seat as Juuarsi sat opposite her.

"So, I bumped up the interview," he said, as Pipaluk stared out of the window. "First Minister?"

"What's that?" she said. "On the bus window — all of them."

"Graffiti?" Juuarsi pressed his face to the window as the driver pulled away from the hotel.

"The same one on every window? It's a stencil of some kind. *Freedom is a lie*," she read aloud as they passed the bus. Pipaluk turned her head. "*Ignorance is darkness.*"

The words were familiar, wrapped around the image of a Greenlandic mask, and covering every window on every bus they passed. Pipaluk saw the same stencil, in various sizes, on every shop, café and office window they passed on the way to the NMG studio. Juuarsi made a note as Pipaluk reached for her mobile.

"She's not answering," she said, tossing her mobile onto her jacket.

"Who?"

"The Commissioner, Petra Jensen."

"Perhaps she's busy, First Minister."

"She'd better be," Pipaluk said, tapping her nail on the window as they passed another bus. "I don't want this to colour the interview. Make sure they know that at the studio."

"I'll talk to the presenter while you prepare."

"That mask," she said.

"Traditional."

Pipaluk checked the date on her mobile. "Tomorrow is *mitaartut*."

"Yes, First Minister."

"So, the mask, Juuarsi, is not coincidental. It's deliberate." Pipaluk swore. "Just when I thought we had got past the whole *Calendar Man* episode. Just when I thought we could relax and enjoy the moment." She sighed. "I just want to enjoy this. Just for a little while."

"It might not be related…"

"No? Overnight, anti-independence graffiti appears on every window in the city. You don't think it's related?"

Juuarsi shrank into his seat, clutching the tablet in front of his chest – a shield against the First Minister's growing fury.

The driver slowed the car to a stop outside the studio, and Pipaluk grabbed her phone, clutching it between her fingers as she pointed at her assistant.

"Get everyone in. I don't care if they are hung-over; I want a full cabinet meeting just as soon as I am done with this interview. And get the Commissioner on the phone."

"Yes, First Minister."

Pipaluk tucked her jacket over her arm, steeling herself in the cold air as the driver opened the door. Juuarsi handed her her shoes and briefcase.

"Call the meeting," she said. "Call the Commissioner."

She didn't wait for his response, Pipaluk stomped through the snow, pulling her jacket around her shoulders as the driver opened the door to the Nuuk Media Group building and held it for her as she walked inside. Pipaluk waited for the security man to buzz her into the studio. She gripped the handle of the door and paused, expelling the irritation from her body, and working her lips into a confident smile as she greeted the presenter's assistant, and let herself be guided to the green room prior to the interview. Pipaluk made herself comfortable, raised her eyebrows in a Greenlandic *yes* for a cup of coffee, and sat down to look through her speech, teasing the appropriate sentences into a highlighted sound bite with a pinch of her finger and thumb. The coffee cooled on the table in front of her and then the assistant called her through to the studio.

"We're recording this segment," she said. "It's good that you came in early. It means we can use more time to edit before we put it out with the main programme."

Pipaluk nodded and sat down in the seat at the desk in front of the cameras. They were smaller than the ones used to record her father's speeches and interviews. It seemed to her that time had shrunk everything, everything but cars. They got bigger each year. *And more expensive.* The thought reminded her that independence meant new trade agreements, and higher taxes, such as VAT. There was a lot of work to be done.

She stiffened at the sudden buzz of an incoming message, glanced at the screen and read the concise morning message from her husband, although it would be midday in Denmark. Pipaluk texted a short reply and turned off her phone.

"All set?" the presenter said, as he sat down beside Pipaluk.

"I'm ready when you are…"

"Klemens Edvardsen," he said, and shook her hand. "I'm new. You're my big break."

"Qitu Kalia hired you?"

"Just before Christmas. I should have been on

the programme earlier, but the Calendar Man affected scheduling."

"He affected everything," Pipaluk said.

"Yes." Klemens swiped at the screen set in a recess in the surface of the desk. "I was hoping to ask you about it."

"Really? I think we should focus on the future, not dwell on the past, Klemens."

Klemens smiled. "How about we settle on the present. We'll take Greenland's temperature and work in some responses from people on the street."

"Have you spoken with my assistant?"

"Yes. He suggested a few things, but I'd like to keep it light and casual to begin with."

Pipaluk studied the man's face, looking for some sign or *tell* beneath his confident and manicured composure. *Qitu chose him well*, she thought, reminding herself that she needed to be careful. The assistant keyed in the intro, and Pipaluk turned to face the cameras, working on her own composure, and the confident smile that would be her signature as she led Greenland into an independent future.

"First Minister," Klemens said, as he turned to face her. "In the interests of cutting to the chase, I'd like to start by getting your opinion on recent events."

Pipaluk scanned his face again before dipping her head in a brief nod. "Of course."

Klemens made a show of reading from his tablet, quoting as he read the first line of the graffiti stencilled across the city, before focusing on the last. "*Ignorance is darkness*. First Minister, do you agree?"

"As you know, Klemens, my party is the most transparent of any Greenlandic political party, past and present. We hide nothing. There are no dark corners to fear, and we fight ignorance with a continued policy of clear and simple language…"

"As simple as the words *freedom is a lie*? That's pretty clear."

"Is it?" Pipaluk leaned into her answer, turning her head slightly for the benefit of the camera, as she composed her response. "It's an ambiguous statement, designed to confuse. Show me the clarity in those words. Better yet," she said, as she straightened her back and looked into the cameras, "show me the people responsible. Let them have their say in a fair and measured debate. This is not the time for confusion or fear. We have had more than our fair share of that this Christmas. This is a time for unity, a time when we need to speak openly, to discuss our fears and hopes for the future of Greenland."

"Yes, but…"

"Just a minute, Klemens," Pipaluk said. She paused to consider what the studio might edit out of the interview, and what they would want to keep. "Let me be clear. Let me be transparent. I only want the best for Greenland, and its people. If someone disagrees, and clearly *someone* does disagree, then let's be open about this. Don't hide in the shadows. There is no reason to hide in Greenland. Not now, not ever. Show yourselves."

Chapter 3

Police Commissioner Petra Jensen missed the first call, and the second. She reached for her mobile the third time it rang, cursing as she pushed it onto the floor. It didn't ring again. Once the room was her own again, she rubbed her eyes and listened to the sound of the neighbours waking, running water through the pipes, calling for a sister to wake a brother to wake their dad. The new family on the floor above Petra's was louder than the one below. They couldn't know that Petra had arranged a late start this Monday morning. She wished she had told them.

Petra pulled back the duvet and slid one leg over the side of the bed. She forced herself to move, rolling onto her side, and pressing herself into a sitting position with a knuckled hand that sank into the soft mattress. She tugged the t-shirt over her stomach, pushed the paperback books on the floor to one side, and stood up. She paused in the hall outside her room to pinch the sleeve of the old and worn police jacket hanging from the peg. She pressed the sleeve to her face, as she did each morning on the way to the bathroom and breathed the smell of north Greenland into her nose. She caught the musk of huskies, the oil of fish, seal blubber and the coppery tang of blood.

"It's alright, David," she said. "It's just a ritual. A little something to remind me of you." She laughed at the books strewn on the bed and the floor – his books. The toothbrush in the glass beside hers – his toothbrush. The jacket – his. The boots in the hall – his, two pairs. The list went on, and she put it to one side, washing her face with his facecloth, and making coffee to pour into David's favourite mug. "I'm working on it," she said, as she blew on the surface of the coffee, rolling her eyes at the thought of David's ghost shaking his head, a wry smile on its lips.

The phone rang again, and Petra ignored it, sipping her coffee as she sat on the couch, her ankles tucked up beneath her bottom, her eyes fixed on the view of Nuuk city docks across the fjord beyond her balcony. She caught a blur of movement and peered through the glass to see the massive carpet-like tasselled shadow of a sea eagle circling above the tower blocks of Qinngorput, just eight minutes' drive from the city centre, and an hour and a half to the summit of Ukkusissaq with its grand views of Nuuk and the surrounding fjords.

"That's why I'll keep the flat," she said, as she finished her coffee.

Petra carried her mug into the kitchen and placed it on the counter beside a thin folder. She tapped the cover, thought of her request for early retirement tucked inside it, and then thought of Aron Ulloriaq, her assistant, and the expression on his face when she had taken it home for the weekend.

"I just need to think," she had said, when she caught him glancing at the folder. "I'll make a decision this weekend. You'll be the first to know."

Once the Calendar Man case had been resolved and the media shifted their focus to the results of the referendum on Greenland's independence, Petra had plenty of time to dwell on the loss of a good police officer – however twisted and corrupted – and her own personal loss of her partner, David. The invitation to spend time in Inussuk was an open one, and Petra drew strength from the thought of fixing up the dark blue house that she and David had lived in, through the good and difficult times associated with their life in the north. She caught a trace of husky in her nose, thought of David's jacket, how he always wore it, on and off duty, in the patrol car, out on the sledge. She was ready to go back, to visit Karl and Buuti, to dip out of the hectic life of a city preparing to enter the global market as an independent country for the very first time.

Petra shook her head at the thought, imagining for a moment the magnitude of the task facing Pipaluk Uutaaq. Eleven years her junior, Petra admired Greenland's First Minister, even if they didn't always get along. It didn't surprise her then, when she retrieved her mobile from between the books on the bedroom floor, that the first call had been from Pipaluk and the following calls were from the First Minister's assistant.

Petra dressed, pinched the sleeve of David's jacket one last time, and then left her apartment. She waited for the bus in a short line of thickly-insulated Greenlanders, their noses, mouths and cheeks hidden behind wool scarves and fleece neckies. Only their eyes were visible, shining brightly, deep within the funnel of their hoods, the tips of the fur ruff flicking in the wind.

The bus was almost empty as the new passengers found their seats. The chatter of greeting and exchange of weekend news rustled through the bus to the sound of zips being opened, scarves unwound, and Velcro tabs unstuck. As the bus drove past the bright lights of the local supermarket the talk changed to that of surprise and exclamation as the lights captured the cautionary stencils on all the bus windows. Petra turned her head, examined the stencil closest to her seat, and then studied the others – identical and numerous. She photographed the one on the window beside her and studied it on the drive into Nuuk.

"Is it just your bus?" she asked the driver, before her stop.

"All the buses in Nuuk. Most of the taxis too."

"When?"

"Must have been early this morning. But it's not vandalism," he said, and pointed at the windscreen. "All the windscreens and mirrors have been untouched. They wanted us to be able to see out. As soon as the boss realised that, he let us drive. It would have taken all morning to clean the windows."

Petra nodded and stepped off the bus. She walked past several windows on her way to the police station and found a smaller stencil with the same letters and motif on the station's ground floor windows. A closer inspection showed the stencil was less defined, perhaps painted in haste, but the station was tagged just the same, just like the buses, taxis and public buildings.

No houses or private cars, she thought, as she entered the station.

Aron met her at the door to her office, took her jacket and hung it on the rack behind the door. He had started doing that just after Christmas, when the initial inquiry had begun to examine the circumstances concerned with Petra shooting a fellow police officer. She recognised Aron's concern, and accommodated his need to protect her.

David would approve, she thought. In his own quiet

way, Aron reminded her of a younger Constable David Maratse, although no-one would ever call David *shy*. Grumpy and withdrawn, perhaps. The thought brought a brief smile to Petra's lips, until she noticed the look on Aron's face, and then she realised she had left the retirement papers on the kitchen counter.

"I forgot them," she said.

"Okay." Aron's shoulders relaxed.

"But I haven't changed my mind."

"Yes, ma'am."

"You know what that means?"

"*Aap.*"

"Right." Petra walked to her desk and sat down. "I have a feeling I know how today is going to go," she said. "But tell me anyway."

"The First Minister's assistant – the new one – has called a few times."

"How many?"

"Six. I think. I may have missed one of the calls."

Petra sighed and then nodded for Aron to continue.

"It's about the graffiti. The First Minister…"

"Wants me to look into it *personally*," Petra said.

"Yes."

Petra tapped the edge of her desk. "Where's Aqqa?"

"Still on leave. He had some overtime."

"He had a lot of overtime, Aron." She tilted her head to one side and looked at him. "So do you."

"Yes, ma'am."

"What about Atii? Is she also on leave?"

"She has some time off, but rumour has it she is doing an evening shift. She swapped with one of the

SRU officers."

"Because he's also overworked." Petra nodded. "I'll talk to the duty officer. Or not," she said, as she caught the brief grimace that pinched Aron's cheeks.

"He does want to talk to you. The department is stretched thin, he says."

"I know. It's been a hell of a December."

"And now that Natuk has gone missing."Aron paused for a moment. "Now that she…"

"It's okay, Aron," Petra said. "I liked her too."

"But what if she was involved, you know, with what Ooqi was doing?"

Petra remembered Natuk's note, rolled up in a cylinder and tucked beside David's gravestone for her to find. There was no doubt that Natuk was involved with the campaign of terror her brother carried out in the run up to Christmas. But to what extent? The details were sparse, and the one person who had the answers, Ombudsman Anna Riis, was proving most uncooperative, due in part to her continued detention at a facility just north of the city centre.

"We might never know. But that doesn't mean we will stop looking. We just need time, Aron."

Petra buried the guilty thoughts of a simple life in the tiny settlement of Inussuk, and hoped Aron believed her. Others might look, but Petra planned to retire, with or without the First Minister's blessing.

"Tell me the rest of the day's schedule – besides the First Minister's graffiti and the duty officer's woes."

"Ma'am." Aron took a breath. "It's not on the schedule, but I thought it was time to visit the detention centre. I could come with you," he said. "I thought we could ask the Ombudsman some questions. If anyone knows where Natuk is…"

"She does. I agree. But she's saying nothing."

"I thought…"

"It's fine, Aron. If there's time, you'll come with me. But let me do the talking."

Petra suppressed a shiver at the thought of Aron blurting out inappropriate questions, and then wondered if she was any different at his age. *Yes*, she realised, *I was*. But Aron's concern was, apparently, boundless, although a little misguided.

Aron excused himself to make coffee and Petra decided to visit the duty officer. She regretted the thought as soon as she entered Tavik Aipe's office. There were red and black stains on Tavik's fingers and the whiteboard was cursed with thick stripes of ink and smudges of names and abbreviations.

"I thought we had a computer programme for that," Petra said, as she knocked and entered the room. The chemical bite of ink pricked at her nose as she perched on the edge of the duty officer's desk.

"It can't cope," he said. "And the boxes are too bloody small." Tavik tossed the red ink pen into the wastepaper basket, cursing as it bounced off the edge and the last drop of ink splashed onto the skirting board. "Sorry, ma'am," he said, as he bent down to pick up the pen.

"It's okay, Tavik."

"No, ma'am, it's not." Tavik capped the pens in his hand and placed them on the small shelf beneath the whiteboard. "This whole Calendar Man incident… it stretched us beyond what's practical. I've got officers calling in sick, all of them are stressed, and some are close to burnout. Royal Arctic has been sniffing around again, trying to poach the younger officers with promises of better pay and much better hours." Tavik slumped in his chair. "I hope you have some ideas, Commissioner, because we're bleeding, and it won't take much for us to bleed out."

Petra thought of the graffiti stencils pasted across the city, and realised Tavik was right, it wouldn't take much at all.

"Talk me through it," she said.

Chapter 4

Custody did not suit Anna Riis. The bed was too hard, the walls too stark. The room lacked even the most basic creature comforts she had spent the latter part of her sixty-two years cultivating in Greenland. Whereas the other ingrates – she refused to call them *inmates* – complained about the DataStream connection rates and restrictions on their browsing habits, Anna missed her throw blankets, the rough base of the kiln-fired mug that prickled the tips of her arthritic fingers, and her bookshelves with the bruised spines of worn and loved books. She missed Shakespeare, and the smell of the print and the pages. Tracing favourite quotes and passages across a screen was not the same. Some things just didn't translate well to the modern age, just like Greenland, and its aspirations to succeed and surpass its colonial status.

"More ingrates," she whispered as she rubbed her fingers and pressed her feet onto the cold cell floor.

She dressed quickly, pressing the creases from her trousers and tugging the hems of her cardigan, before crossing the floor to tap the screen hanging on the wall to confirm the time of the meeting with her lawyer. She had thirty minutes before breakfast, and one hour to kill before Mia Kiberg talked her through the statement she was to give about her relationship to Ooqi Kleemann, the so-called *Calendar Man*, deceased, killed by a bullet from the Police Commissioner's gun, and the shotgun blast from Petra Jensen's pit bull, Gaba Alatak.

"Ooqi," she said. "My little Ooqi."

The walls were too slick and white to absorb the name, and it hung there, in the air above her bed, as

Anna smoothed the sheets, folded them beneath the mattress, tutting as she tugged and tucked the loose corners into place.

She paused as the memory of a younger, carefree Ooqi flickered into her thoughts. She remembered the press of his knees and his bottom on her thighs as he wriggled onto her lap to listen to one more story before bedtime. At twelve, he was too big for her lap, something his sister, Natuk, reminded him of, chiding him in Greenlandic, until Anna opened the first page of her beloved bard's most famous comedy and began to read.

"*If music be the food of love, play on.*"

That was Ooqi's cue to stop fidgeting, and Natuk would drift from the doorway to Anna's feet, twisting the ends of her long black hair into her mouth and then curling them around her fingers as she listened. Anna did her best to read each part with a different voice, eliciting giggles from Ooqi, and reluctant smiles from his sister. Anna knew the lines off by heart, allowing her to peer over the book and catch the creases at the corners of Natuk's mouth, until the girl emerged from the layers of trauma from her childhood, relaxed and listened and laughed.

It was on Anna's lap and at her feet that the twins travelled to distant lands, discovered politics and the natural law and order of government, the intrigues of deceit and the consequences of action and inaction. It was a master class in manipulation, and once the challenges of the language were overcome, Ooqi and Natuk absorbed each lesson and quizzed Anna to a degree which delighted her, and, through some of Natuk's more astute enquiries, titillated Anna's fundamentalist ideals.

The seeds were sown, quietly cultivated.

It was Anna who encouraged the twins to work hard at school in Denmark. She pushed them equally hard at home, spending her own money on private tuition to ensure that they did not lose their mother tongue, and that they understood the power of language.

It was Natuk that imagined a Greenlandic Shakespeare – a complicated plot with characters tugged out of the crevices in the granite, magma-hot, moulded and beaten into twisted personages until they cooled and were ready to enter the scene, stage right and stage left. They would swoop from the eaves and crawl out of trapdoors, masked, bent, hideous to look at, like the shaman's *tupilaq*. Anna could not read the words, but the crude images Natuk drew of each character appalled and enthralled her.

"Who is this?" she asked, perhaps a year before Natuk and her brother returned to Greenland, to finish their studies at a Greenlandic gymnasium.

"That's the king of Denmark."

Anna peered closely at the figure, nodding as Natuk tapped the king's warped crown with the tip of her finger.

"Is he a good king?"

"He's the best," Natuk said. "But the people don't know it. They have lost their way, and he needs help to help them understand."

"Lost their way? How?"

"They have turned their back on him."

"Hm."

Anna rarely made sounds, and Natuk lifted her head to study her foster mother's face.

"Grunting is for animals," she said, repeating one

of Anna's oft-quoted comments.

"Sound is for words and song," Anna said, and smiled. "You're quite right." She smoothed her hand through Natuk's hair, pulling her close as she sat down beside her. "Tell me more about your play."

The plot was at once complicated and compelling, as was to be expected from a student of Shakespeare. Anna listened as Natuk explained what happened, to whom, and when. The conclusion was tragic and poignant. It sparked a cascade of thoughts and ideas in Anna's mind, a world of possibilities, a trigger to be activated if necessary.

"When necessary," she said aloud, and the walls of the cell replaced the more comfortable and intriguing borders of her memory. Anna lurched from Natuk's teenage attempts at Greenlandic Shakespeare into her present confines of detention. The knock on her door, the crack of the hermetic seal as the door opened, and the curt command to attend breakfast came shortly after. Anna slipped on her soft laceless shoes and followed the guard along the corridor to the canteen. The sounds of plastic plates sliding onto plastic tables drifted along the corridor towards her, souring Anna's thoughts as she imagined the taste of plastic food on her tongue.

The human grunts, farts and breakfast belches over pallid plates of reconstituted eggs and tired bread, pressed Anna further and deeper into a sense of depression. This was detention. This was her penance for the crimes of passion and preservation. Passion for her country and its protective and protectorate ideals to preserve a society, its people and its culture. *Ooqi had given his life for these people*, she thought, as she stood in line for her breakfast. *And still they had turned their back on him, and the king of Denmark.*

"Ingrates," she whispered.

"What's that?"

It was the guard. Female. Short and stocky. A Greenlander. Short black hair. Glasses. A photo fit caricature of the many Greenlanders over forty. Anna tried not to sneer, but she felt her lips crease, and blamed it on the eggs.

"Nothing," she said, and carried her tray to an empty table.

Breakfast was followed by obligatory recreation, the polishing of the wooden floor of the handball court in the centre of the detention centre. They polished it each day for forty minutes. Polished it until it shone. It was so slippery she doubted it would ever be used for training or even the promised tournaments, regularly advertised on the cell media screens. But the shush of the dry mop on the wood was therapeutic, and Anna imagined the rocky Illyrian coastline, or the battlements of Elsinore castle, until a shrill whistle announced that the day's recreational requirements had been met, and all inmates should return to their cells.

Anna pressed her mop into the clasp on the wall and followed a guard to one of four meeting rooms. She waited for a second as the guard entered the code for the door, and then stepped inside.

Mia Kiberg was half Anna's age, and worth less than half the money Anna paid for her services. Any other lawyer, she believed, would have found just cause for bail, and Anna would be preparing for her hearing at home, rather than in the custody of the Greenlandic Prison Service – a poor model of the superior Danish institution.

Any further thoughts Anna had were dispelled as Mia tried to break the ice with morning pleasantries.

"Have you had coffee?" Mia asked. "I've arranged for coffee."

"I prefer tea," Anna said.

"Of course." Mia gestured for Anna to sit. "I've run through your statement and had my colleagues in Copenhagen look at it." She placed a tablet on the table in front of Anna. "We've made a few revisions."

Anna skimmed the document, and then tapped the screen to close it. She pushed the tablet towards Mia.

"I'm not saying that."

"What part?"

"Any of it," Anna said. "Revisions? You've changed everything."

Mia nodded as she sat down. "Yes. My colleagues and I…"

"Who?"

"Sorry?"

"Which colleague? Was it Harfeld?" Anna pointed at the tablet. "It doesn't read like Harfeld. If he had been here, I would be home by now."

"Anna…"

"Who was it?"

Mia sighed. "It was me."

"You made all the revisions?"

"Yes."

"You didn't even show it your *colleagues*, did you?"

"Yes, I did. And they agree with me. We believe it is important that you adopt a more conciliatory tone."

"Conciliatory?"

"Less offensive."

"I didn't feel I was being offensive."

"You are *on* the offensive, Anna. It makes it difficult to argue your position of *not-guilty* in connection with the Calendar Man case."

"It wasn't me placing the bodies on the streets."

"I understand that. But it would help your defence if you adopted a more empathetic tone. Less accusatory."

"You're going to have to explain that," Anna said. She folded her arms across her chest.

"Your initial statement, the notes you gave me – there is a sense of satisfaction in the events to which you are being linked, by association."

"They didn't listen," Anna said. "They didn't try to communicate."

"With who? Ooqi Kleemann? You see, Anna, that's what makes it difficult to represent you here. By all accounts, and with the Jonkheer's statement…"

"The Jonkheer?"

"Yes. It's Coenraad Kuijpers' statement that has made it so difficult to have you released prior to the hearing." Mia paused as a guard entered the meeting room carrying a tray of coffee. She waited until she was gone before continuing. "The Jonkheer's testimony will be the most difficult to argue against. He says it was your idea to wage a campaign of terror to alter the outcome of the referendum."

"An outcome he desired."

"And admits to," Mia said. "But it doesn't change the implication that you inspired Ooqi Kleemann – your foster child for several formative years."

"Formative?"

"That's what the prosecutor will say, Anna. They

believe you encouraged Ooqi Kleemann to procure dead bodies and instil fear and chaos to disrupt the voting. We believe they will suggest and try to prove that you not only encouraged Ooqi Kleemann, but that you trained him, and ordered him to influence the referendum."

"Hm," Anna said.

A stray thought pricked at her conscience, reminding her that *grunting is for animals*.

"Ooqi Kleemann is dead, Anna."

"You don't have to remind me of that."

"No, I don't. But it's important that you understand that prior to his death, and before the police realised his involvement in the case, he was a respected young police officer. There are some within the police department, that even now express regret for his death. They are looking for some measure of understanding; one might even call it sympathy."

"You're talking about the Police Commissioner," Anna said.

"Amongst others, yes, that's correct."

"Her sympathy is misguided. Her regret is just another word for guilt. Ooqi was twice the Greenlander she will ever be, twice the *human*. Petra *Piitalaat* Jensen killed my little boy, and she will pay for that." Anna stood up. She slapped the coffee mug with her hand and it shattered against the wall. "Just wait," she said. "Petra Jensen is going to pay. They all will."

Chapter 5

The image of Tavik's whiteboard schedule lingered as Petra walked back to her office. She heard the metallic clack of equipment as she passed the Special Response Unit's ready room. She resisted the impulse to check-in, concerned that she might see the same lines of fatigue that stretched the skin around the duty officer's eyes and tugged at his cheeks. But then she heard a familiar voice, and Atii stuck her head around the door.

"Commissioner," she said, as she stepped out into the corridor. "How are you, Petra?"

"I'm fine, Atii."

"We missed you at New Year's."

"I know. I wanted a quiet evening."

"Who with?"

"No-one," Petra said, and smiled. "Well, I tried reading one of David's books. And then I spent most of the night telling him just what I thought of science fiction. Honestly, budget reports are lighter reading."

"Petra." It was Atii's turn to smile.

"Yes?"

"Come inside and have a coffee. You need to be around people."

"Not ghosts, you mean?"

Atii shrugged and nodded for Petra to follow her inside. If anyone new to the department wondered at the informality of their relationship, an old hand would mention the name Gaba Alatak, and, once the newcomer connected the dots and they realised that Atii was Gaba's wife, a wave of understanding would wash over them. Petra might be the Commissioner, but Gaba was a living legend in the Greenlandic police force. Arrogant, with an ego like an upturned iceberg with the tip hidden just beneath the surface. Atii had married Gaba only a few years after the Commissioner had ditched him. It was public knowledge, as was Gaba's service record. It made sense that the Commissioner had chosen him to accompany her when she tried to arrest the Calendar Man, although the board of inquiry might disagree.

"How's Gaba doing?" Petra asked, as Atii poured her a coffee. The five men and women of the SRU continued to check their gear once they had acknowledged the Commissioner's presence.

"You mean with the inquiry? He's fine. It's not the first time he's been roasted for his actions."

"But it's the first time as a civilian."

"He's pleading self-defence." Atii frowned. "I'm surprised you haven't heard."

"I have a meeting at the end of the week. They're keeping me in the dark until then, I suppose." Petra gestured at the team. "What's all this? Routine?"

"Partly. I think we're going to get a call pretty soon."

"About what?"

"The First Minister was interviewed this morning. The presenter is new. He pushed her about the graffiti all over town."

"I haven't heard it yet," Petra said. "I had a meeting with Tavik."

"Right," Atii said. "Well, she's called a press conference. Âmo security has been paid until the end of January, but I want to be ready. Just in case."

"Is there something you want to tell me?"

Atii picked up her mug and nodded towards her office at the rear of the ready room. Petra followed her inside. There was a moment of quiet as the SRU team members stopped working. Atii frowned at them, and then shut the door.

"They're just grouchy," she said.

"Tired?"

"Pretty much bombed, like the rest of us. But they don't get paid to sit on the sofa."

Petra waited as Atii walked around her desk. The wheels on the chair squealed as she pulled it out and sat down. Petra ignored the chair in front of the desk, choosing to lean against the wall instead. Atii took a sip of coffee, and then began.

"Gaba has been nagging me for days to tell you about this, but I've got nothing conclusive, no evidence."

"Tell me, Atii."

Atii nodded. "Commissioner," she said, changing the tone of her voice. "I don't think we've heard the last of Ooqi Kleemann."

"He's dead, Sergeant."

"*Aap*, I know, but that's not what I mean. I think there's more to this."

"More? It was a pretty elaborate terror campaign. He had us running all over the city."

"He did, but I don't think he acted alone."

"You're talking about Natuk?"

Atii nodded. "She was his brother, something they kept hidden from all of us. Why?"

"That's a question for the Ombudsman, Anna Riis." Petra put her mug down on a shelf. "Although, I can't imagine she will tell us anything. Aron suggested I visit her later. Perhaps you want to come with me?"

"No," Atii said. "I need to be in the city. I want

to be available if something happens." She shrugged. "*When* it happens."

"You think Natuk is still in Greenland?"

"I think she could be anywhere, but I'm betting she's close. Gaba is tired of hearing about it. He says if I'm so sure of it, then I should get permission to go looking for her."

Petra laughed at the look on Atii's face. She imagined the discussion Atii had with Gaba, and his exasperation. She'd seen a similar look on his face, all too often. There was a reason those two were made for each other, once an idea took hold, neither of them could ever let it go.

"Are you asking for my permission, Sergeant?"

"Yes, ma'am. I want to start a search for Natuk Petersen, starting with a wide sweep of Nuuk, Little Amsterdam, and Chinatown."

"We're quite stretched at the moment, Atii."

"We are."

"I'm not sure we have the resources."

"What about Aron?"

"My assistant?"

"He spent time with Ooqi. I think they were friends. Rumour has it that he was quite taken with Natuk, although he was too shy to do anything about it." It was Atii's turn to laugh. "That's probably a good thing. Anyway," she said, "he's pretty competent with computers, whereas my guys are all action. I think Aron could narrow the search parameters, lighten the load."

Petra remembered Aron picking up the slack when Ooqi disappeared from the Calendar Man task force, revealing a quiet technological confidence that amused Petra. It would have confused David, despite his interest in science fiction.

"Don't work him too hard," Petra said, as she moved towards the door. "And keep me posted."

"Thank you, ma'am."

Petra's mobile buzzed as she left Atii's office. She slipped it out of her pocket as she walked along the corridor, answering it with a swipe of her thumb as she reached the bottom of the stairs.

"Commissioner Jensen?"

The accent was American. Petra pressed the phone closer to her ear and stepped to one side to make room for two officers and a young man with a t-shirt spattered in vomit.

"Yes," she answered, in English.

"My name is Joshua Seabloom. I'm the new station Commander at the USCG base in Nuuk. I wondered if we could meet."

"I'd like that," Petra said.

"How about now? I'm right outside."

Petra turned to face the main entrance and saw a tall man in uniform wave from where he stood behind the glass. Petra ended the call and walked to the door. She nodded for the officer sitting at the security desk to buzz the Commander into the building.

"I'm sorry to come unannounced," Seabloom said, as he walked past the security guard. He shook Petra's hand, and then stamped the snow from his boots on the rough mat in front of the door.

"It's fine," Petra said, as she studied the Commander. The grey tinge to his closely-cropped hair suggested they were the same age, but his height made him look younger. He was almost as tall as Gaba. She felt a brief flood of heat to her neck and tugged at her collar. The Americans changed Commanders at the base faster than the Chinese changed security officers. The previous Commanders had been too busy to make an impression, but Petra thought she might just remember Joshua Seabloom.

"Are you alright?" he asked.

"Yes, I'm fine," she said.

"You're sure? You look a little flushed."

"I'm fine." Petra gestured towards the stairs. "Shall we meet in my office?"

"Yes," he said. "I'll follow you."

Aron looked up from his desk as Petra entered the outer office. He stared at the American until Petra waved her hand in front of his face, and gestured for Seabloom to wait for her inside.

"Aron," she said. "Can you find us some coffee?"

"Yes, ma'am."

"And," she said, as he turned away.

"*Aap*?"

"Sergeant Napa needs your help with something. Don't let her work you too hard."

Petra waited until Aron was busy with the coffee before joining Seabloom. She found him studying the map of Greenland hanging on her wall.

"It's such a huge country," he said. "And now, with the retreating ice sheet, it's just getting bigger. Huge potential for real estate," he said, and grinned.

"But still no roads," Petra said.

"Yeah, that's an issue, right there."

Seabloom hung his winter coat on the stand beside the door and sat down at the table. Petra waited for Aron to bring the coffee. She took the tray from his hands, placed it on the table, and then closed the door.

"This is unusual," she said, as she poured the coffee. "We don't usually hear much from your side of the fjord."

"We're good at that," he said. "We want the world to adopt our ways, buy all our products, and leave us the hell alone." Seabloom grinned. "Does that fit?"

"A little." Petra laughed. "How can I help you?"

"Actually, I've come to help you." Seabloom tugged a medium-sized tablet from his jacket pocket and placed it in front of Petra. He tapped the glass and swiped an image until it filled the screen. "You've got an epidemic," he said, as Petra stared at a photograph of the graffiti she had seen on her way into work.

"It's on the to-do list," she said.

Petra leaned back in her seat. She took a sip of coffee as Seabloom selected another image from a folder and enlarged it.

"What about her?" he asked. "Isn't she one of yours?"

The image of Constable Natuk Petersen in uniform, her long black hair tied in a ponytail at the back of her head, jolted Petra's thoughts from the graffiti to the all too familiar scene of Ooqi's death, when she pulled the trigger of her pistol and Gaba blasted him with his shotgun. Petra replayed the scene often, in the quiet, empty moments of her flat when David's ghost allowed her. There was a moment during each re-enactment, when she remembered Ooqi placing his glasses on the table, recording his last moments, and she wondered just how many times Natuk had watched her brother die.

"What's this about?" she asked.

Seabloom poured a dash of cream into his coffee and crumbled a cube of sugar onto the surface. He looked at Petra as he stirred it, nodding at the tablet as he started to speak.

"We have several cutters based at the station in Nuuk. One of them is a little old now, a National Security Cutter called the *Stratford*. She was on her way back from a patrol when she spotted a Greenlandic trawler that wasn't trawling."

"What do you mean?"

"It was behaving erratically, as if the Captain was asleep at the wheel. The *Stratford*'s Captain hailed the trawler, and, when she received no response, she sent a boarding party across to inspect the boat. The crew were not asleep, but there was a heated argument below decks. The boarding party made the crew aware of their presence," Seabloom smiled. "They might have fired off a round or two – there was quite a ruckus. Anyway, once they got the crew's attention and identified the Captain of the boat, they interviewed him. The trawler was based in Nuuk but had just dropped someone off in Ilulissat. The Captain was pretty pissed about it. He said his boat had been commandeered by a police officer. One of the crew took that picture when your officer wasn't looking." Seabloom took a sip of coffee. "I thought you might want to know."

"When was this?"

"December twenty-third."

Petra looked at the image of Natuk, picturing for a moment her escape from Nuuk, on the same day that Petra killed her brother.

"What has this got to do with the graffiti?"

"The same crewman who took the picture said

that he heard Natuk muttering something as she forced the Captain to sail north."

"Forced him?"

"The crewman said her pistol was unholstered, and that she seemed agitated. He said she repeated a phrase a couple times: *darkness is ignorance*. Or something like that. I wouldn't have thought any more of it, until someone tagged the bridge across the fjord with that stencil, and the same words. One of my ensigns made the connection. He was on the *Stratford* that day, and he reported it to his Captain, and she reported it to me." Seabloom leaned back in his seat and crossed his legs. "Now, I don't know the circumstances. I arrived just after Christmas, so I've only been here a few days. But I understand you had a situation over the holidays, and that things got quite out of hand. Once we put these things together," he said, as he swapped the image of Natuk with that of the graffiti, "I thought it best to come straight to you. Then I saw the same image all over town."

"You think Natuk is connected to the graffiti?"

"I think it's a good bet. Don't you?"

"My SRU leader thinks so," Petra said. She took a long breath and looked at Seabloom. "Thank you for this."

"You're very welcome."

Petra watched as Seabloom finished his coffee. She frowned as he poured another.

"What?" he said. "Only one coffee per meeting?"

"No," she said. "I just thought you would be leaving."

"I told my driver I would be at least an hour. Your coffee is stronger than ours; I thought I'd have another cup while we discuss matters."

"What matters?"

"In the interests of international relations, I'd like to offer my assistance, and," he said, with a nod towards the tablet, "from the looks of things, I think you might just need it."

Petra swiped the tablet to look at the image of Natuk one more time, remembering Tavik's whiteboard and his fractured schedule of tired officers.

"Yes," she said. "I think we might."

Chapter 6

Natuk surprised the small group of men and women assembling drones with a second visit. She moved between the tables with barely a nod of acknowledgment as the last components of each drone was assembled and they were put to one side to make space for the next. The parts were mostly plastic, and the sound of a metal click, and clack caught Natuk's attention. She moved away from the drones and watched a young man assemble a pistol. She pulled it from his hands as he slid the magazine into place.

"You don't need it," she said, reducing the pistol to a pile of components and an empty magazine in just a few seconds. The man stared at her as she flicked the bullets from the magazine with her thumb, one by one, as she returned the man's stare until he withered to a safer distance and pressed his back against the wall.

"We won't win this campaign with bullets and guns," Natuk said. She tossed the magazine onto the table and took a moment to look at each of the men and women at the tables. There were five of them, including Assa, the man that had unlocked the door on her first visit earlier that morning. The late morning sun pressed at the edges of the metal plates covering the broken windows and burned window frames. "To get the outcome we want, to truly move the people, we have to let them lead. All we have to do," she said, with a nod at the drones on the tables, "is show them the way."

"You want to change people's minds with a few drones?" The man leaning against the wall pushed away from it and squared his shoulders. "It won't make a difference."

"Each drone has a camera. Once this thing kicks off, we feed those images – all of them – into the DataStream, hacking into the mainstream media, the independents, even the government channels. It will be a feeding frenzy, and we need to keep them hungry."

"Them," the man said. "Just who are they? Eh? You don't even know them."

Natuk glanced at the leader of the group, the man with the keys.

"You told me to find people to assemble drones," Assa said, with a shrug.

"I assumed you would find believers," she said.

"Hey, I believe." The man pointed at the two men and one woman standing between the tables. "Just ask them."

"What's your name?" Natuk asked, as she took a step towards the man.

"Qallu."

"And what do you believe in, Qallu?"

"The same as everyone else," he said. He waited for Natuk to respond, continuing when she didn't. "I want a strong Greenland, one my children can be proud of."

"But not you?"

"Not right now," Qallu said. "Right now, we're weak."

"And your children?"

"I don't have any yet."

Natuk picked up the magazine from the pistol. "Tonight, you're going to forge a new direction for your country. Would you want your children to know you did it with a gun, or that you inspired people – young Greenlanders, the future – that you inspired them to rise up and make a stand?"

"But it's not a new direction. Is it?" he said. "You're trying to change the vote, to keep us under Danish rule."

"Not rule," Natuk said. "Just under their wing, just a little longer, until we're ready to forge our own path."

"Under their wing?" Qallu laughed. "Under their thumb, more like."

"So, you want freedom, Qallu? The kind Pipaluk Uutaaq says she can give you?"

"At least she keeps her promises. She did what she said she would do, what her father said *he* would do. She got us this far, even when that crazy Calendar Man ripped through Nuuk with his…"

The words died on Qallu's lips as Natuk placed the pistol magazine quietly on the table and took a small step towards him.

"I don't think," she whispered, "you're the best fit for this operation, Qallu."

"It's a job," he said. "I did this for the money."

"There's no money," Natuk said.

"What?" Qallu looked around her. Natuk moved to block his view of the other people in the room.

"We do this because it's the right thing to do, Qallu. We do this because we believe Greenland needs protecting, and we're not ready to go it alone, not yet. Maybe one day. Soon, I hope. You want your children that see a truly independent and free Greenland? So do I. I look forward to that, Qallu, I really do. But right now, you have to decide what role you will play in Greenland's future."

"What role?"

"You said you believe. You said you wanted a stronger Greenland, a country your children – the ones you hope to have – can be proud of. So, I ask you again, Qallu, what are you going to do about it?"

Qallu frowned. He focused on Natuk's face, on her eyes, and he missed the subtle shift of her stance, the slight bend to her knees, the flattening of her palms and the straightening of her fingers. He missed all the signs that hushed the other people in the room.

"Listen," he said, as he tried once again to look around Natuk. "I'll just take my money and go."

"There's no money," Natuk said.

"Then I'll just go," Qallu said, as the hush finally reached him, and the cool air inside the room settled between them.

"Not before you answer my question."

Qallu stiffened. He straightened his shoulders, clenched his teeth and stared down at Natuk. She had seen it before when on patrol, especially on Friday and Saturday nights, that moment when *they*, usually a man, attempted to dominate the situation, confusing assertiveness with arrogance as they reassessed the distribution of power, scoffing at the sight of the woman in front of them, perhaps a head shorter than they were. Natuk could forgive the drunks their moment of manliness. But even though Qallu was not drunk, he made the same mistake as men often do, he forgot that when the roles were reversed, women tended to skip over the testosterone pump and bristle, and strike, hard and fast. Just as Natuk did, slamming the blade of her right hand hard into Qallu's collar bone. She pinned him against the wall, trapping his left arm against his body as she punched him three times on the side of his face with her left fist. The small ridges of her knuckles, like tiny granite peaks, dimpled Qallu's cheek as he groaned and slumped against the wall.

"You're weak," she said, as she lowered her fist, gripped Qallu's jacket and lifted him. "Just like Greenland. "How long do you think we would last with people like you at the helm? Tell me that, Qallu."

"Just let me go," he whispered. "Let me go."

"After you've seen all this?"

"I won't tell anyone."

"It's not that simple," Natuk said, as she let go of Qallu. He slid down the wall to slump at her feet. Natuk turned her head to look at the others in the room. She caught Angut's eye as he entered the store, locking the door behind him. "A minute ago, Qallu was ready to use a gun to force the people to change their minds, but he can't even defend himself. Do you really want a man like that carrying a weapon?"

Qallu squirmed as Natuk pressed the toe of her boot into his stomach. He slid across the soot-black tiles, inching towards the door at the rear of the store as Natuk spat on the floor.

"Violence doesn't work," Natuk said. "Fear doesn't work." Natuk glanced at Angut. "It's been tried. You all know what happened this Christmas. The referendum went ahead anyway, because the voters were not informed. They were just *told* what was best for them. Some ideological idea was dumbed-down and served. There was no information. Tonight, we're going to change that. We're going to *inform* the people, the youth of Greenland. We are going to give them the power to…"

Natuk paused at the sound of a door opening.

She flicked her head to look at the rear of the store, saw the door creak to a close, and then heard a second door slam. She heard the crunch of a table behind her as she raced into the back room and Angut barged passed the drone assembly line. She held out her hand as she reached the back door and Angut pressed her pistol into her hands. She slid it into her jacket pocket as she exited the store.

"I'll go around front," Angut said, as he scanned the short alleyway behind the store.

"No," Natuk said. "He's still here."

"I don't see him."

"Shush. Listen."

A raven cawed from the roof above them, claws clacking on the metal gutter. Natuk ignored it, focusing on the garbage piled against the alley wall, waiting for collection. She pulled the pistol from her pocket, gripped it in two hands, and walked forwards. The raven cawed again, flapping its great wings in protest as Natuk kicked at a pile of cardboard boxes, scattering snow and paper waste to reveal an empty hiding space.

"I was sure he was still here," she said.

"He ran," Angut said. "You scared him pretty good." He nodded at the electric motorcycle leaning against the wall. "So much, he didn't even take the bike."

"Shit."

Natuk kicked at another box and then slipped the pistol inside her pocket. The raven cackled on the rooftop. Natuk glared at it.

"I'll find him," Angut said.

"*Naamik.* I have another job for you." Natuk took a last look at the raven and then nodded for

Angut to follow her to the end of the alleyway. "I need you to pick up my mother."

"Your mother?"

"Foster mother."

"Okay, where is she?"

"She is in the detention centre. Her name is Anna Riis."

"Natuk…"

"Yes, it *is* possible. Once I ignite the city, you'll have plenty of time to get in and get her out. Assa will help you bypass security. I've already patched him in through a back door breach. The police will have their hands full. Just get her to the boat, and then come and find me."

"And what will you do, about him?" Angut said, with a nod towards the street. The sun had brought out the mid-morning shoppers, and their increasing numbers slowly replaced the last of the late-night revellers.

"Once I float his picture in the DataStream, I'll let the people bring him to me."

"And if they don't?"

"They will, Angut. Have a little faith. This is an important night. We need to trust the people to make it *their* night. As soon as they feel they own it they won't let anything jeopardise it, and our work will be done."

"Huh," Angut said. "They'll still need a leader. If it's not going to be you, then who?"

"I've found someone," Natuk said. She smiled at the memory of the few hours she had spent with Tiina Markussen. Brief but enjoyable. Tiina had speed-talked for two hours without a break, hiding her nervousness with passionate strains of patriotism, balanced with the need to do things at the right speed, with the right foundations. Natuk had guided her with a measured comment her and there to keep her on course, to strengthen the pillars of her foundations, supporting her fundamental beliefs that Greenland would be independent when the time was right, and not before.

"The girl at the nightclub?"

"*Aap.*"

"And you can trust her?"

"She's committed, Angut. She understands, perhaps even more than we do. The people will respond to her, and *her* people, her generation, even more so."

"What's her name?"

"I'm going to call her Viola, and by the end of the night, all of Greenland will know her, and the young people of Nuuk will follow her, all the way to the end."

Angut laughed.

"What?"

"The light in your eyes," he said. "It's so bright, it's like they're on fire."

"And?"

"Just don't let it go out."

Chapter 7

Viola. The name was as exciting as it was unfamiliar, Tiina thought, as she boiled water for tea in the closet-sized kitchen of her one room apartment. She waited for the water to boil and stared at the sofa bed pressed into the corner of the room. The duvet and blankets were ruffled, and her pillow still had the shape of Natuk's head. If she pressed her nose to the pillow, she could smell her shampoo. Tiina closed her eyes and remembered their hushed conversation, Natuk's soft lips pressed to her ear, nibbling her lobe when she expected a response from Tiina. It had been hard to breathe, and it had nothing to do with Tiina's asthma, or the radiators turned up to the max. It was as if Natuk's presence stole the air from her lungs, she kept her breathless, feeding Tiina with small pockets of air, between words, between promises sealed with kisses.

Soft lips.

Sharp teeth on her lobes, her lips.

The scratch of clipped nails across Tiina's skin, tracing the shape of her ear, removing her librarian-thick glasses, such a cliché.

"I can't see without them," Tiina had said.

"You don't need to see. Just listen, feel, smell, taste," Natuk had said. "Use your senses. Let go."

Tiina gasped at the memory, and the bubbling of the water popped against the side of the pan, splashing on the hotplate, tugging her back into the moment. But the thought of Natuk, just a few hours earlier, stayed with her, and the smell of the tea, a cinnamon blend, jolted another thought, the soothing caresses Natuk had given and the gentle words she had said after they had used each of the senses to explore all of their bodies.

"You will be Viola," Natuk had said.

"*Viola?*"

"It's your new identity."

"Don't you like my name?"

"I love your name, Tiina, but you can't be Tiina Markussen tonight. I need you to be Viola, from now until the end."

"What end?"

Tiina remembered Natuk's touch, the way she curled Tiina's hair through her thin fingers, tucking errant lengths behind Tiina's ear as she leaned in to whisper.

"The course we are on is not healthy, it is not free. Viola needs to change that. Viola can change it, with my help."

"Viola can?"

"*Aap.*"

"How?"

That was when Natuk had stood up, the blanket slipping from her body as she leaned over the table, the one Tiina studied at, and plucked the mask from the wall. Natuk lifted it in front of her face, found the string and tugged it over her head. She stood there, her face hideously masked, her naked skin warm in the last glow of Christmas lights. Natuk danced, lifting one leg high, bent at the knee. She straightened her arms, swung her forearms at right angles, dangling like a puppet as she alternated the high steps, first her left leg, then her right. Her small breasts barely moved, the triangle of thick hair between her legs was dark in the shadows as Natuk twirled out of the light. There was more hair and more shadows beneath her arms, adding to the magic and mystery of the masked dance. Tiina was captivated, her lungs caught between breathless gasps and heaves of laughter. She knew the game. She knew what was required of her. It was *mitaartut*, when Greenlanders in masks and padded clothes knocked on doors and danced their way inside people's homes, carrying a skin drum, challenging them to recognise them, hitting them with the drumstick if they didn't. Natuk being to tease Tiina, grasping a pillow and beating her with it until Tiina held up her hands and danced around Natuk and into the kitchen where she found a bag of sweets, spilling them into Natuk's hands and onto the floor, carrying on the tradition with the gift of candy, as she pretended not to know Natuk's name.

"Kiss me," Natuk said.

"No, not with that mask."

Natuk lifted the mask over her face, letting it rest on her head, the hideous chin just above her thick black brows.

"Kiss me, Viola," she said.

Tiina remembered the kiss, the touch, the taste of Natuk's skin, and she remembered the mask. She carried her tea into the room and found the mask on the table. She put down the mug and carried the mask to the bed. It was black as soot, with thick red paint accentuating the contorted shapes and curves that distorted the face around the eyes, puffed the cheeks beyond the chin, and spread the mouth. The teeth were chiselled, wood-grained with a splash of yellow paint. Tiina pressed the tip of her finger into the thin hole cut between the top and bottom row of teeth. She remembered Natuk's pink tongue peeping through it, remembered the taste of it.

Tiina flopped back on the bed, closed her eyes, and sighed. This was love. She was sure of it. And she would do anything and everything for it. For just one more dance, with or without the mask.

"I am Viola," she whispered. "I am yours to command."

Natuk's first command had been for Viola — not Tiina — to attend the First Minister's press conference, to use her student journalist credentials to sit at the back, and to ask a specific question, to be brave, and to insist.

You speak for your generation, Viola. You are their voice.

That was the last thing Natuk had written in the DataStream, just half an hour earlier.

Viola got up off the bed. *Viola* changed out of her pyjamas and t-shirt into jeans and a body-hugging fleece. It was *Viola* that practiced her question in front of the bathroom mirror, and *Viola* that switched her librarian glasses for the slightly thicker rims of Natuk's glasses, the ones she had slipped on Tiina's face when she left her apartment.

"Now you can see," she had said, "and I will show you the world."

The lenses were expensive, adjusting and auto-correcting to accommodate Tiina's reduced vision.

"Not Tiina," she reminded herself. "I am Viola."

Viola flicked her eyes around the lenses, testing the functions of each icon, trying the blink, track and slip method of retinal navigation. It was awkward and exciting. She felt free, she felt whole, and, she realised, she felt empowered.

An icon in the bottom field of the right lens flashed, and she blinked it into the centre. The image window had a reduced opacity, and Viola walked from the bathroom to the kitchen, looking through the image and reading it simultaneously. She smiled at the thought that – glasses on – she was Viola. She removed the glasses for a second, wondering who would return.

"Still Viola," she said, and pressed the glasses onto her face.

The window was a message box, and she read the message confirming the time and place of the First Minister's press conference. Viola finished dressing, laced her quilted boots and grabbed her jacket. She was crunching through the snow on the footpath outside her apartment just a few minutes later.

She saw the graffiti on the bus, focused on the stencil on the window closest too her, and blinked as the glasses scanned the image, triggering a stream of data that cascaded down the left lens of her glasses. Viola slowed the stream with the blink and track technique. She transferred one item in the stream onto the right lens, positioning it with another blink. The stream in the other lens slowed as Viola focused on the right, holding her breath as she read the confirmation from the team leaders that the preparations for *mitaartut* were in place, and that they were waiting for further orders.

The words *Viola will confirm* flickered onto the lens at the bottom of the message.

Who?

Viola. Wait for her signal.

"My signal?" Viola whispered.

She glanced at the other passengers on the bus. She relaxed. Viola, it seemed, was just as anonymous and unremarkable as Tiina Markussen. It was no wonder the team leaders did not know who she was.

Nobody did.

But all that is going to change, Viola thought, as the bus slowed for her stop. *Natuk said so.*

She flashed her student card at the entrance to the community centre opposite the supermarket on the main pedestrianised street curving through Nuuk's city centre. She found a seat at the back, as instructed, and blinked the question onto the lens of her glasses, as instructed. She looked up at a hush from the audience, and the click and hum of cameras and video recording equipment.

Before her alter ego, before Natuk, Tiina had always been in awe of Greenland's First Minister, impressed by her commitment, her clothes, and, not least, her confidence. Pipaluk projected all three as she walked up to the podium in front of the journalists, politicians, and business men and women gathered for her press conference.

"Thank you for coming at such short notice," Pipaluk began. She waited a beat, letting the audience settle as she sought out the camera. Pipaluk pressed her slender hands around the sides of the podium and leaned forwards, ever so slightly, but enough to change the pitch of her voice. It was strong, balanced, determined. "Christmas is nearly over," she said. "Tomorrow is *mitaartut*. Our decorations must come down, according to tradition. But that doesn't mean that we are finished with our celebrations. It does not mean we must put the past behind us. No," she said, and shook her head. "Now, more than ever, it is important to remember our past, and to draw on many lifetimes' of experience, the good, the bad, even the memory of those times that have terrified us." She paused to look at the people in the audience. "This

Christmas was one of those terrifying experiences, and I don't imagine anyone will ever forget it. But that doesn't mean we can't move on. It doesn't mean we are weak. No-one should imagine we are weak, and we must be strong, even in the face of uncertainty." Pipaluk took a sip of water and the journalists in the front row tapped a few notes into their tablets. "Many of you will have seen the graffiti on the windows of the buses and taxis this morning. You will have seen the same graffiti on the windows and walls of public buildings, your favourite café perhaps, or plastered across the library. Someone, perhaps lots of people, want you to be scared again, as if the Calendar Man or something like him has returned, and the question of our independence and freedom is in jeopardy. Well," Pipaluk said, "I'm here today, speaking to you now, to tell you that the Calendar Man is dead, and that the people of Greenland have voted. The darkness is retreating, and there is no ignorance. Not anymore, and never again," she said. "Now there is light, hope, and freedom." She smiled, relaxed her grip on the podium and looked at the camera. "This is a time for hope. Hope makes us strong, and together we are stronger."

Several in the audience clapped. Viola felt her heart race under the soft salvos echoing around the room.

Now, Viola.

The text flashed onto the lens.

You're not alone. I am with you. We all are.

"Any questions for the First Minister?"

Viola didn't see who asked. She closed her eyes for a second as she stood. When she opened them, she saw two of the three cameras pointing at her. She saw her image, her face, flash across the lens of her glasses, and she saw the DataStream spike with a stream of comments and her name tagged to her image.

"Yes?" Pipaluk said. "You have a question."

"I do, First Minister," Viola said.

"What is your name?"

"My name is Viola," she said, "and I represent my generation, and all the generations of Greenland."

"Okay," Pipaluk said. "And your question?"

Viola took a breath. Her glasses registered a flicker of movement to the right of the podium, zooming in on the raised thumb of a young man, followed by the brief nod of his head. He mouthed the name, *Viola*, and she smiled.

"My question, First Minister," she said, "concerns the future of Greenland, and everything you have done to undermine it."

Traffic in the DataStream spiked for a second time, and the heat from the lights threatened to overwhelm her. And it might have, if she had been Tiina. But she was Viola now, the voice of her generation. The DataStream slowed to a stop, and even the hum of the video cameras was hushed as everyone in the room, everyone in Nuuk, and the whole of Greenland waited for her to speak.

Chapter 8

Pipaluk waited until her assistant confirmed that the press was gone and slammed the door to the room reserved for staff at the community centre. The thin walls shook and the last of the Christmas decorations shivered against the walls, the red paper star knocked against the window pane.

"Who the hell is she?" Pipaluk said, whirling on her assistant.

Juuarsi started to speak, and then tugged his tablet to his chest as Pipaluk gripped the back of one of the chairs and ripped it out from beneath the table. She sat down, pressed her palms flat against the table edge, and glared at him.

"Well?"

"She said her name was Viola."

"I know that, Juuarsi. I was there. Remember?" Pipaluk took a breath. "I want to know her real name, the one she signed in with."

Juuarsi checked the tablet. The tips of his fingers squealed across the glass as he scrolled through the list of attendees registered before entering the hall for the press conference.

"It's not here," he said.

"Not possible. She had to show I.D. to get into the hall."

"I know, but she's not here." Juuarsi held out the tablet and waited for Pipaluk to take it. "Either she wasn't registered, or her name has been erased."

"Find out," Pipaluk said, as she pressed the tablet into Juuarsi's hands.

He paused at the door. "Can I get you anything, First Minister?"

"Her name," she said. "Now go."

Juuarsi shut the door quietly behind him. When he was gone, Pipaluk slumped in the chair, closed her eyes, and teased her fingers through her hair. She ran the Q&A session through her mind as if she had instant playback. She pictured Viola, trembling as she stood, and someone passed her a microphone. The trembling stopped with Viola's first words.

"My question, First Minister," she had said.

Pipaluk didn't want to hear it again. She checked her thoughts, but the words filtered through, anyway, echoing around her head: *undermine, undermine, undermine … Greenland's future.*

She remembered the heat in the room, the cameras – she imagined the lens pressing against her face, boring into her eye, rooting around her mind in search of an answer.

"I'm sorry," Pipaluk had said, "what did you say your name was?"

"Viola."

"Just *Viola*?"

"*Aap.*"

It was a coping mechanism, a strategy she had learned to employ, to buy time. Everyone in the room knew it, and it would be dissected now and for the days to come by the media. *What did she have to hide?* They would ask. *Is she undermining Greenland's future? How?*

How was the question Pipaluk wanted to ask. *How did this* Viola *get into the press conference? Who was she and who put her there?*

Pipaluk recalled the second stalling strategy, knowing that it was dangerous to ask the young woman to clarify the question – the repetition was another sound bite for the media, but she needed time to think, to respond to the woman.

Girl.

Viola looked like she was barely in her twenties.

The memory of the moment, the repeated question, the spike in viewers, the explosion of comments and the buzz on the streets, made Pipaluk's head ache. She pressed her hands to her eyes, pressing harder as she remembered her non-committal response, hoping the pain of the pressure against her eyes would erase the memory.

It didn't.

Pipaluk saw the slack jaws and wide eyes of the press and Nuuk's most influential business men and women as she turned to Viola and said, "Get out. I don't have time for babysitting ill-informed students, *Viola.* I suggest that next time you sneak into a press conference, you spend a little more time preparing your questions. Do your research, because questions like that truly will undermine the future of our country."

Viola had said nothing for a moment, and Pipaluk wondered if she was communicating with someone. The lenses of her glasses were thick, but even from her position at the back of the room, Pipaluk could see that Viola's gaze was steady and trained on her.

"Is that your answer, First Minister?"

"It's all you're going to get from me today."

Pipaluk remembered gripping the podium, in preparation of another rebuke, if it was necessary. But the girl simply zipped her jacket, slid out of the row of seats, and walked slowly to the door. The cameras followed her, as if the lenses were glued to the girl's body with thin filaments of spider silk. It was the same with the audience, as the girl turned their heads; they were all caught in her web. Pipaluk could almost see it, could almost grab it, but she dared not, for then she would be caught too. She chose to flee instead, leaving the podium and exiting the stage just as Viola closed the door of the hall behind her.

"Damn it," Pipaluk said, as she slipped her hands down her cheeks and into her lap. She let her head droop, felt her chin in the space between her collar bones. Her hair tickled her cheeks and she felt them flush with blood and heat and the sheer bloody ignorance of the girl.

Ignorance is darkness. ·

It was happening again. Someone was trying to derail Greenland's push for independence, and it made no sense. This is what they wanted, what they voted for – a clear majority. But someone, somewhere, wanted a different outcome and they had chosen this *girl* to speak for them.

Cowards, she thought. And then: *Who is she?*

"First Minister?" Juuarsi said, as he opened the door.

"What?"

"Have you got five minutes for Sergeant Atii Napa?"

Juuarsi opened the door at a nod from Pipaluk, and Atii squeezed into the room. She tucked her fingers between her jacket and vest and waited for the First Minister to look at her.

"Do *you* know who she is, Sergeant?" Pipaluk said.

"That's not why I'm here." Atii glanced at the window. "It's hot in here, First Minister. Do you mind if I open the window for a second?"

"Whatever," Pipaluk said and waved her hand.

Atii opened the window just a crack and only for a second, but it was enough to catch Pipaluk's attention as the sound of chanting rose from the street outside. Atii closed the window and pointed at the crowd gathering between the community centre and the supermarket.

"That's why I'm here," she said. "First Minister, I'd like your permission to escort you home."

"I'm staying at the suite at the hotel," she said, and pointed towards the Hotel Hans Egede sign just visible through the window at the end of the street. Her face paled as she realised the crowds had effectively blocked her route to the hotel.

"It might be better if you went home, instead."

"It's being refurbished. Everything is packed in plastic. It's been like that since the end of November."

"I understand," Atii said, "but given the circumstances…" She paused.

"I want to go to the suite."

Atii nodded and pressed the radio microphone clipped to her vest. "Bring the car around the back. We're going to the hotel." She looked at the First Minister. "As soon as you're ready."

It took less than three minutes for Atii to get the First Minister and her assistant inside the police car parked at the rear of the community centre. Pipaluk ducked her head as she climbed into the back. Juuarsi sat next to her, still gripping his tablet. Pipaluk almost laughed, and then she saw the crowds, as the driver began to edge the car out of the alleyway towards the street.

"Stay down, please," Atii said, with a glance over her shoulder. Pipaluk ducked her head. "It's going to get a bit bumpy. But don't be alarmed. The glass is thick enough to stop bullets."

"Have they got guns?" Juuarsi said, his voice was shrill compared to the chanting of the crowd, the thumps of their palms on the glass and the taunts and jeers – strong enough to pierce the bulletproof glass.

"This is ridiculous," Pipaluk said. "The hotel is right there."

"Twenty metres," Atii said. She flinched as someone threw a plastic bottle of cola against the windscreen. It bounced off the roof. The second bottle was glass, and it smashed on the bonnet of the police car. "Keep moving," Atii said, as the driver touched the brakes. "Don't stop. Just keep it steady."

Pipaluk looked up as Atii undid the snap securing her pistol in the holster strapped to her leg.

"Sergeant," Pipaluk said.

"Not now, First Minister."

"You have my permission to fire on the crowd, Sergeant."

Atii shifted her gaze between the crowd bumping and pressing the car as the driver inched towards the hotel.

"With all due respect, First Minister," Atii said, "that's not your decision to make."

"But these people are threatening my life, Sergeant."

"They are making your life uncomfortable. I agree."

"What are you going to do about it?"

Atii leaned forwards, tapped the driver on his arm, and pointed to the right.

"Sergeant?"

Pipaluk turned her head at the wail of sirens descending on the hotel from both directions, two cars on each side of the street. She watched as they slowed to let officers out of the back. As the police interlocked their riot shields, the cars peeled off to the sides, blocking the road and forming a channel through which Atii guided the driver. The shouting and jeering grew louder, and several glass bottles smashed against the police shields, but the thumping and jostling of Pipaluk's car stopped as the police forced the crowd away from the vehicle.

"That's it. There's your space," Atii said. "Go."

The driver floored the accelerator, forcing Pipaluk and Juuarsi back into their seats, as he raced through the police cordon, swerving around the first taxi in the rank outside the hotel entrance, and darting through the gap between the hotel and the shops beneath the five floors of rooms.

"Slow it down," Atii said, as she gripped the door handle. "Now stop," she said. "Stop."

A gust of wind caught Pipaluk's hair as the passenger doors burst open and two members of the SRU pulled the First Minister and her assistant out of the car. A third SRU officer, armed with an assault rifle, watched the crowd from his position at the rear of the car. Pipaluk resisted the urge to complain at the police officer's grip on her arm and let him drag her inside the rear entrance of the hotel. His partner pushed Juuarsi through the same door a second later.

"You're safe, First Minister," Atii said. "Now, if we can just get you to your room."

"I want guards on the door," Pipaluk said, as Atii guided her through the lobby and into the elevator.

"And I want to speak to Commissioner Jensen."

"Yes, First Minister." Atii pressed the button to close the elevator door as soon as Pipaluk's assistant was inside. Pipaluk noticed the Sergeant's hand had not left the grip of her pistol, but that the weapon was still inside the holster.

"Who were they?" Pipaluk asked, as Atii led her out of the elevator to her suite at the end of the corridor.

"We don't know yet."

"Why don't you know?"

"The situation is developing, First Minister," Atii said, as she knocked on the suite door. The police officer inside stepped to one side as they entered.

"That's not good enough, Sergeant."

"Please feel free to complain," Atii said, as she turned in the middle of the room. "I'm sure my boss will take your complaint very seriously."

"Seriously? Sergeant…" Pipaluk said. The words froze in her mouth as she looked around Atii and noticed the man and woman seated at the table by the window.

"First Minister," Petra said, as she stood up. "I'd like to introduce Commander Joshua Seabloom from the United States Coast Guard; he has something to tell you."

Chapter 9

Petra stood to one side as Joshua Seabloom pulled out a chair for the First Minister, poured her a glass of water, and fixed her a smaller, stronger drink from the mini bar. His charms were not lost on the First Minister, and Petra frowned at an unfamiliar feeling that caught her unawares, something she hadn't felt in a long time, a pang of jealousy. Petra almost missed Joshua's initial outlining of their shared concerns for the safety of the city's residents, as she dealt with another feeling, stronger than the first, it cut deeper, right to the bone.

I feel guilty, she thought. *David. I feel guilty because of David.*

Petra dismissed the thought. Now wasn't the time. Joshua caught her eye, and she nodded for him to continue.

"I had my tech guy at the base analyse the stencil. I take it you've seen it?"

"They're all over the city," Pipaluk said.

Joshua nodded and picked up his tablet from the table. He swiped an image of the stencil onto the screen and enlarged it.

"The cultural stuff I'll leave to you," he said, "but technically I can tell you that the stencil was printed from a template on several 3D printers. We've analysed about fifty of the images. A lot of them match, with the same tiny striations – especially along the curved edges. Here and here," he said, as he pointed at the screen. "We found four separate stencil patterns, suggesting four different printers. Considering the reduced flights over Christmas, and the lockdown you had because of the Calendar Man incident, we're guessing these printers are located in the city, and that the template was downloaded to them."

"It couldn't just be four different stencils printed from one printer?" Pipaluk asked.

"No," Joshua said. "Like old fashioned laser printers and even typewriters before them, they are unique, especially if they have been damaged, or tagged by the manufacturer – something so tiny it can only be discovered with intense magnification, and time." He smiled. "My tech guy at the base has plenty of time."

Pipaluk reached for the glass of water, and then pushed it to one side in favour of the clear spirits and the soft splintering of the rough chunk of glacier ice bobbing within it. The ice clicked on the bottom of the glass as Pipaluk finished her drink. She placed the glass on the table and looked at Petra.

"We agree with the Coast Guard," Petra said, taking her cue. "Given the extent of the graffiti that has been spray-painted all over the city, we believe there are many stencils in play, which would suggest that lots of copies were made from each printer." She took a breath. "It also means this is well coordinated, with many people involved. To cover all the public windows and the windows of all the buses and taxis in one night, we estimate there has to be at least forty people working through the night."

"Forty people who are trying to derail Greenland's independence," Pipaluk said. She reached for the shorter glass, tapping her fingernail against it as she remembered it was empty. "What about this girl? Viola?"

"We have a name, based on her photo – we had a

hit from the University database. She studies journalism. Her name is Tiina Markussen."

"Markussen?"

"No relations of interest," Petra said. She waited for Pipaluk to look at her before adding, "We do, however, think she might be connected with someone we are very interested in."

"Who?"

"Constable Natuk Petersen," Petra said. "She went missing shortly before we tried to apprehend Constable Ooqi Kleemann."

"Constables," Pipaluk said. "Both of them."

"Yes."

Petra glanced at Joshua as the First Minister stood up. She wondered what he knew of the Calendar Man case, and how much she should tell him. She was reluctant to tell him too much, not only because it was embarrassing that two officers with the Nuuk Police Department were responsible for creating such chaos in the city, but also because she liked Natuk and Ooqi. Regardless of what Ooqi had done and what Natuk might be doing, Petra was sad that the department had lost two competent and intelligent officers. *Perhaps too intelligent*, she thought. *And yet not intelligent enough to know when they were being used and manipulated.* Petra chided herself at the thought; Ooqi and Natuk were children when Anna Riis took them in. *And what's my excuse? I was an adult when they used and manipulated me.*

A light touch on Petra's arm made her look up. Joshua showed her his mobile and then pointed at Pipaluk standing at the window.

"I have to take this," he said.

"I'll talk to the First Minister."

Joshua walked to the adjoining room and closed the door. The door muffled his response as Petra walked over to Pipaluk. She smiled as the First Minister continued to talk in English as if Joshua was still in the room.

"Petra," she said, "I'm sorry about my quip about your Constables. I do realise they acted alone, or together." She frowned as she turned to look at Petra. "However they acted, the Calendar Man brought this city to a standstill, and he was just one man. You think there are forty people running around Nuuk, tagging all the public buildings?"

"At least," Petra said.

"And why only the public buildings?"

"I think they want to keep the people on their side. They can't do that if they deface private property."

Pipaluk pressed her hand to her mouth as she looked out of the window. It was still light, and the police on the street below were clearly visible as they mopped up the last of the protesters and sent them on their way.

"They look tired," she said.

"They are."

"And you, Petra. Are you tired?"

"Yes, I am." Petra gestured at the door to the room Joshua was using to take his call. "That's why I'm pleased the new Commander wants to help."

"And why is that?" Pipaluk asked. "Forgive me, Petra, but I *am* a politician. What does he want?"

"Want?"

Pipaluk placed her hand on Petra's arm and smiled.

"There are times when you are gorgeously naïve,

Commissioner. You do your job, and you ignore politics as much as possible."

"Politics gets in the way of policing, First Minister."

"You're right, and until now it has been Danish politics determining what happens with Greenlandic policing, but once Greenland is independent, Petra, you'll have to deal directly with me and my staff, with policies that affect Greenland *directly*. I wonder, can you do that?"

Petra thought about her retirement papers in the folder on the kitchen counter. She had read through the fine print. All that remained to do was sign them. Even Aron, her assistant, was ready for her to sign, as if his need to process paperwork overruled his previous concerns about Petra leaving her post.

"I'm ready to do what I have to do, for as long as I have to do it," Petra said.

"I'm glad, Petra," Pipaluk said.

They both turned at the click of the door opening, and they both watched Joshua stride across the room to the join them.

"They've blocked the bridge," he said.

"What bridge?" Pipaluk asked.

"The one across the fjord to the Coast Guard base. It's off limits, as you know. I have two Seamen and a Petty Officer squaring off against a group of about thirty Greenlanders in their late-teens to mid-twenties. They commandeered a bus. They are right outside the guardhouse." Joshua stuffed his mobile into his pocket and reached for his winter coat draped over the back of one of the chairs at the table. "My men are following protocol and Standard Operating Procedures," he said.

"Which means what, exactly?" Petra asked.

"It means, if the crowd doesn't back down, they will open fire with warning shots. After which, if there is no sign of de-escalation and they consider themselves and their position to be under continued threat, they will defend themselves, and they will shoot to wound, before shooting to kill."

"You can't kill Greenlanders in Greenland, Commander," Pipaluk said.

"It's alright, First Minister," Petra said, as she caught Joshua's eye. "I won't let him."

Petra felt a surge of strength, the same kind that flooded through her body each time she realised that the time for discussion was over, and definitive action was required. She glanced at Atii, caught the subtle dip of the Sergeant's head, and then turned to the First Minister.

"Sergeant Napa has arranged for security, you'll be safe here," she said. "Commander?"

"Yes?"

"Can I escort you to the bridge?"

"Escort me? Hey, Petra, this is your shitstorm, I don't need *escorting* anywhere. It's your people on the bridge. Your responsibility. My men – they're *my* responsibility. You can escort me to the bridge, or you can drive me there, but it has to happen now."

"Agreed," Petra said. "Let's go."

Atii caught Petra's arm as she walked out of the suite and into the corridor. Joshua continued to the elevator.

"What is it, Sergeant?"

"We're stretched pretty thin, ma'am," Atii said.

"I know, Atii."

"I can talk to Gaba... He's started recruiting

already to expand his team."

"No, Sergeant. We've already eaten into next year's budget. Until the situation demands otherwise, we're going to have to manage with what we've got."

"*Aap*, ma'am."

Petra nodded towards Joshua as the elevator doors opened. "I have to go."

"SRU will meet you at the door. They'll *escort* you to the bridge," Atii said, and grinned.

"Thank you, Sergeant."

Petra lost count of the graffiti obscuring windows and blistering the sides of the buildings they flashed past in the small convoy of police cars. The same police officers that cleared the protesters from the street outside the hotel were jammed into the back of each car, helmets in their laps, flak vests and additional armour pressing into their joints. Petra glanced over her shoulder at the two men and one woman on the back seat.

"Busy shift," she said.

"Yes, ma'am," the female officer said.

Petra pressed her palm against the dashboard, bracing as the driver flung the car around the last corner before accelerating towards the bridge. The wheels spun for a second on a smooth patch of ice. The driver recovered, grinned at Petra, and then increased speed.

"SRU have tactical command," Petra said to the officers on the back seat. "The Americans are concerned about the security of the base. We need to get you between the protesters and the guardhouse."

Petra waited for the officers to respond and then looked out of the windscreen. The group had swelled to about sixty young Greenlanders and two buses, their collective breath hung in a cloud above them as they chanted and waved banners and placards. Petra recognised the mask from the stencil, and, as the driver slowed, she noticed that several members of the crowd were wearing actual masks. She wondered if Natuk was among the crowd, and the thought propelled her out of the vehicle as the driver slid to a stop.

"Commissioner, stop."

An SRU officer leaped from the car in front of Petra's, curling his arm around her as he pulled her to the rear of the vehicle. Joshua climbed out of the passenger seat and joined them a moment later.

"I need you to wait here, ma'am," the SRU officer said. "Just until we get a perimeter set up."

"She might be here," Petra said, and pointed at one of the masked protesters.

"Who are we looking for, ma'am?"

"Constable Natuk Petersen."

The SRU officer nodded, raised his arm and spun one finger in the air instructing the police officers to form up and link their shields. He pressed the submachine gun to his chest and raised his voice as the crowd turned to face them.

"I'd like you to get in the car, ma'am," he said.

"I'm staying right here."

"I can't leave you here alone, ma'am. Atii will have my balls."

"She's not alone, officer," Joshua said. "I'll stay with the Commissioner. Now go do your job, before my men are forced to do theirs."

Petra almost laughed as the two men glared at each other, but a sudden flash of black above her head and the buzz of quad motors caught her attention, and Petra stared at the sight of a sleek drone equipped with a bank of camera lenses.

"That's one of yours," Joshua said. "Right?"

"Not ours," Petra said.

She glanced at the crowd, flicked her gaze across the faces – with and without masks – and then stared at the drone. With no proof, and little more than a fisherman's word to suggest Natuk Petersen was in Greenland, Petra couldn't shake the feeling that the renegade Constable had just arrived.

Chapter 10

Natuk leaned between the two Greenlanders sitting at the table along the wall, the bank of computer screens lit their faces with a stream of code cascading down the right-hand side of the screen with real-time drone feed windowed on the left. She pointed at one of the windows.

"Enlarge that one," she said.

The window expanded to fill the screen and the image of the bridge across Kangerluarsunnguaq Fjord sharpened. Natuk tapped the screen to focus on one section of the image and the camera on the drone zoomed in. She smiled when she recognised the mask from Viola's apartment. *Viola*, she could have named her Jeanne d'Arc, but the Shakespearian name was more familiar, and it suited her purpose. Viola was in disguise; her true intent was hidden. Natuk corrected her thoughts; it was Natuk's true intent that was disguised. For the moment, at least.

"Pull back and pan to the right," she said.

The blue emergency lights of the police cordon flashed and swirled across the faces of the protesters, illuminating the masked and unmasked protesters alike. Natuk tapped the screen again, zooming in on the police officers assembling their shield wall. She tapped the screen, pinched the image of two faces standing at the rear of a police car, the one furthest from the protestors. Natuk slid her finger and thumb across the screen and the faces sharpened, she could almost hear the drone clicking through the focus range of its camera. Then she paused and took a step back from the screen as the face of Police Commissioner Petra Jensen overlapped the other feed from the drone's camera array.

"*Piitalaat*," she whispered. "That's what he called you."

"What's that?" said the Greenlander to her right.

"Nothing," Natuk said, as she pointed to the adjacent screen. "Give me the image of the man standing next to the Commissioner." She waited as the man's white face filled the screen. "Enhance and save a copy. Cast it to me. Good. Now run it through the identification suite. I want to know who he is."

Natuk pulled her glasses from her pocket and put them on. She blinked her way through the start-up icons, scanned her messages and then swiped the image of the man onto the left lens as she studied his career and biography details on the right. Commander Joshua Seabloom, age fifty-two, was married with three children, the eldest of which was about to start high-school. He owned a modest house on East Cherry Street, not far from the USCG Seattle Base on Alaskan Way. Natuk scrolled though the details with an upwards flick of her eye until she found what she was looking for. She nibbled at her lips, clamped the tip of her tongue between her small white teeth and blinked to zoom on one particular detail. According to the details gleaned and assembled from open sources and the USCG magazine and New York Times articles, Seabloom was a Coast Guard Intelligence Officer. Natuk tasted blood on her tongue, swallowed and blinked an icon to the right of Seabloom's details to begin a deeper background scan. *You might be trouble*, she thought, and wondered why he should be assigned to Nuuk now, and what his real purpose might be? Base Commander might be a significant rung on the promotional ladder, but the modest house on Cherry Street, Squire Park, suggested that promotion and moving up the ladder were not the kinds of things to motivate Seabloom. Natuk decided he could be dangerous, detrimental to her plans, but there was nothing more to do until the scan was finished. Natuk looked at Seabloom's image for a few seconds, appreciated the handsome cut of his jaw and the steel glint in his eye, and then blinked the image into a folder.

She reached up to remove her glasses, and then stopped, remembering one more thing she had to do before she returned to the drone feed from the bridge. Natuk searched for the image she had captured of Qallu and pasted it onto the message boards for her network of enthusiastic young Greenlanders in Nuuk and tagged the image with a high-priority search icon, something to occupy the more passive *truth seekers* not currently involved with the protest on the bridge. Of course, once they found Qallu, it was up to Natuk to deal with him. She slipped her hand around the grip of the FNS compact pistol in her jacket pocket and removed her glasses.

Natuk walked back to the table and watched the drone feed from the bridge. One of the cameras was programmed to seek and follow exaggerated activity, and it zoomed onto a scuffle at the shield wall. The image blurred for a second as the drone responded and flew to a better position to observe and record the first line of protesters bashing their fists on the police shields. A second camera zoomed in on the Coast Guard officer and his men standing in front of the guardhouse. Natuk noted their weapons were drawn, as was Seabloom's. She snapped her head to the left as the drone beeped a warning through the computer speakers. There was a flash and the camera angle wobbled for a second as Seabloom fired three bullets at the drone.

"Send another drone," Natuk said.

She knew the ballistic armour of the drone was capable of withstanding more than a few shots from a handgun, but she didn't want to miss anything from the bridge. The live feed she pushed into the DataStream was valuable propaganda that she would use to incite more young, impressionable Greenlanders out of their homes and onto the streets. And now, thanks to Seabloom, shots had been fired. The situation had just escalated.

Natuk frowned as she wondered why he would do that. Then she saw a hand raised in front of his face. She leaned forwards, pressed her finger and thumb onto the screen and zoomed out, just as Petra pressed her hand on Seabloom's arm and he lowered his weapon. Natuk flattened her lips into a thin smile. It was a nice show for the cameras, something she would edit in the DataStream. She would twist the Commissioner's concern over the use of firearms with the video footage of her brother's death. The image of the Commissioner holding her pistol in two hands as she murdered Ooqi Danielsen was a powerful one, something Natuk could use, no matter how painful the memory.

"I think you should see this," said the taller of the two Greenlanders.

"What?"

"You told us to fix her image and build into the drone's facial imagery software."

"*Aap.*"

"The woman."

"Viola," Natuk said. She looked at the third screen as the Greenlander tapped it.

A group of protesters had turned away from the Nuuk police, as if they had realised that the police were trying to get between them and the Americans. Viola was just visible at the head of the group, fist raised, and a confident energy in her stride. She seemed to draw power from the mask and was channelling it into her legs as she strode across the bridge towards the guardhouse. *This isn't the time for martyrs*, Natuk thought as she saw the Coast Guard officer order his men to ready their weapons. Assault rifles would make short work of Viola and the small group of protesters that had split up from the main demonstration.

"Where's that other drone?" she asked.

"On its way."

"Not fast enough."

Natuk gripped the back of the Greenlander's chair and wheeled him away from the table. She slid the keyboard across the table and hunched over it, the keys cowered beneath the stab of her fingers, as the windows of footage from each camera fused into just two feeds – one of Viola and her small group, and a close-up of the Americans on the other.

There was a hush inside the store, punctuated by the staccato commands Natuk punched into the keyboard and the imagined burr of the drone's propellers as it churned through the frigid air above the bridge into a position between the two groups.

The first flashes of gunfire obscured the camera image focused on the Americans. The drone rocked as a volley of bullets threatened to knock it out of the sky.

"ETA drone two?" Natuk said as she shifted her focus from the images on the screen and the keyboard.

"Eighteen minutes. There's a headwind."

"Too slow," she said, and cursed. Natuk grabbed the Greenlander by the shoulder. "Take over. Keep that drone between Viola and the Americans, and the second one, when it gets there." Natuk moved away from the table, pulling her glasses from her pocket and slipping them over her nose as she ran to the back door.

"What are you going to do?"

Natuk didn't answer. The door slammed against the wall as she burst into the alleyway. Natuk leaped onto the back of the motorbike, pressed her knees against the sides as she checked the battery and short-circuited the power sequence with a blink of the emergency start-up icon in the right-hand lens of her glasses. The rear wheel spun until the Natuk depressed the ice spikes with a flick of a switch on the handlebars, and then she buzzed down the alleyway and onto the street.

As soon as she was clear of the pedestrian street, Natuk cursed at the lack of gloves and hat as the cold air rushed against her exposed skin, biting at her earlobes and pinching her fingers. She raced through the city, blinking the drone feed onto the lens. The drone was lower in the sky, jerking upwards with bursts of power as it laboured under the repeated onslaught of Coast Guard bullets. But the Americans had done two things right, at least. Viola's group had stopped and was huddled at the side of the bridge, and, behind them, it was just possible for Natuk to see the protesters renewing their assault on the police, invigorated and incensed by the gunfire.

Natuk flashed through Little Amsterdam and Chinatown as the road dipped down to the fjord. She stopped the bike short of the bridge, two hundred metres from the police cordon and the shield wall. Natuk tugged the pistol from her pocket and held it in a loose grip at her side. She felt a rush of cold air over her head at the same time as a new feed patched into the stream of data on the lenses of her glasses. The second drone had arrived and started harrying the Americans. The last image from the first drone showed Viola running away from the Americans. Natuk scanned the crowd and used her glasses to identify Viola. She fixed her with a targeting crosshair as she inched the bike towards the police cordon.

"Don't turn around," she whispered, as she saw Petra's long hair twisting in a cold draught barrelling up the fjord. "Not now."

The police beat the protesters back against the side of the bridge, leaving a gap between them and the police cars, wide enough for Viola to slip through if she took it, if Seabloom and the Commissioner didn't stop her. They were the only ones between Viola and Natuk.

Natuk gripped the throttle on the handlebars with one hand as she aimed at the rear window of the police car, just to the right of Petra's head. *Just a distraction*, she thought, although the temptation for murder and revenge made her finger tremble and she had to fight to steady her aim.

"Viola," Natuk shouted, as she fired her first shot. She gunned the bike forwards as the bullet shattered the rear window of the police car. "Viola, run."

Seabloom slipped on the ice as he dragged Petra to the ground, pressing his body over hers as Natuk accelerated onto the bridge. Natuk turned her head away from Petra, stuffed the pistol into her pocket and wrapped her arm around Viola's slim waist. She dragged her onto the bike, clutching her to her chest as she turned the bike. The heels of Viola's boots scraped across the ice as Natuk accelerated.

There was a shout, in English, a deep American voice that fit so well with the chiselled image of the Coast Guard Intelligence Officer. The shout was followed by a warning shot. Natuk anticipated the hot fire of impact, waited for the second when she would be thrown from her bike and the plans she had for Greenland's Twelfth Night, *mitaartut*, would be over, spoiled in a sprawl of bodies and blood beneath a bike on the bridge. But there was no impact, and no further shots, just the squeal of tyres and the wail of the police siren that blistered across the fjord.

Natuk glanced at the drone feed in her glasses, saw Petra behind the wheel of the police car and Seabloom holstering his pistol as he climbed into the passenger seat. Natuk grinned as she helped Viola into a more comfortable position on the bike. She corralled the second drone with a series of blinks, slaving it to her bike, and flicked the feed onto the left-hand lens as she accelerated up the hill and away from the bridge. The drone followed the police car, as Petra and Seabloom chased Natuk back to the city.

Chapter 11

The electric SUV was faster than Petra anticipated. She spun into the first corner, forcing Seabloom to press his hands against the dashboard as she corrected, downshifted, and powered out of the corner and into the straight leading into the city. Petra could feel the smile tugging at the corners of her lips, curling her mouth upwards. She wondered if it was appropriate and realised that she didn't care. A combined effort of sickness, grief, terror and concern had kept Petra bottled up for most of November and December, it was time to let go, to let it out, and to get results. Petra's smile stiffened as she thought about the result she wanted most, in that moment, as the motorbike leaped ahead of her and charged into Chinatown. In the adrenaline-spiked moment between Seabloom knocking her to the ground and the girl jumping onto the motorbike, Petra had caught a glimpse of the biker's eyes, and she thought she recognised them. Such intelligent eyes, almost obscured behind think-rimmed glasses. She had seen them before – the same eyes and the same glasses. The rider might have blonde hair, but there was no mistaking the family likeness – Petra was convinced she had just seen Ooqi's sister, at large and alive and dangerous in Greenland.

In my city, she thought, as she reached for the radio.

"Wait a second," Seabloom said, as he leaned back in his seat. "You want to tell me what's going on?"

"We're in pursuit of a person of interest."

"I can see that," he said, "and I can feel it with

every corner." He held his breath as Petra accelerated through a gap between a bus and a delivery van. "But I need to know why we left my men on the bridge to chase a blonde on a bike?"

"She's not blonde."

"Yes, Petra, she is. I saw her."

"I mean it's not natural. She's dyed it."

"Who has?"

"Natuk Petersen," Petra said, with a quick glance at Seabloom. "The young Constable your man learned about. The one in the picture you showed me."

Seabloom frowned for a second, and Petra waited as he recalled the image of the woman he had shown her.

"Think about her stature," Petra said, as she saw a space in the road up ahead and slipped the SUV into it. The emergency lights flashed along the side of a second bus, lighting the faces of the passengers peering past the graffiti on the windows for a better look at the chase.

"Yeah, okay," Seabloom said. "Suppose it is her. What was she doing on the bridge?" He twisted in his seat to look out of the shattered rear window. "And who the hell is controlling these drones?"

"It has to be her," Petra said. "And I think that young woman is the key."

"The one clinging to the front of the bike? It's a wonder she hasn't fallen off."

"No, it's not," Petra said. "Natuk won't let her fall."

Seabloom leaned back in his seat as Petra tugged the radio handset off the dashboard.

"You admire her," he said.

"Yes."

"Regardless of what she may or may not be involved in?"

Petra nodded and pushed the button to transmit.

"This is Commissioner Jensen. I need a roadblock between Chinatown and Little Amsterdam. Two female suspects. The driver has blonde hair, and the passenger is wearing a mask – traditional, Greenlandic. The passenger might be Tiina Markussen." Petra paused. "The rider is Constable Natuk Petersen."

There was a crackle of static as Petra clipped the old-fashioned handset into place and pressed the button for hands-free.

"Ma'am, this is Sergeant Napa."

"Go ahead, Atii."

"Did you say the rider is Natuk?"

"I believe so, yes."

There was a pause, and then Atii's voice burst through the radio chatter. Petra imagined her running as she heard the Sergeant's breathy response.

"On my way."

Petra stomped on the brakes as a group of Chinese miners wobbled into the street. Natuk disappeared into the distance, the glow of the motorbike's taillight merged with red, yellow and orange dragon tails stretched across Chinatown's main street.

"You don't have a helicopter?" Seabloom asked, as Petra weaved around the miners.

"There's no budget for that."

Seabloom reached into his pocket and pulled out his mobile. He glanced at the drone pacing the SUV as he dialled.

"Put me through to Wilkie in the hangar."

"Wilkie?" Petra said.

"Yes." Seabloom smiled. "I think you might have met his mother when you were attached to Polarpol."

"That was a long time ago," she said, as she drove beneath dragon's tails on the main street. "How do you know about that?"

"It's my job, Petra," Seabloom said. He smiled for a second as the Seaman in the hangar connected his call. "Wilkie? I need you to spin up the chopper. We've got an active manhunt in the city. You'll be coordinating with the local police. Alert the airport and let me know when you're in the air."

Petra pulled over to the side of the road. The drone hovered three metres ahead of them, its cameras fixed on the windscreen. Seabloom's fingers twitched as he pocketed his mobile and reached for his pistol.

"It won't do any good," Petra said.

"I know, but I really want to shoot it." He looked out of the windows. "Why have you stopped?"

"I lost her when the miners drifted into the road. I thought we would wait for the helicopter. And she might double-back once she hits the roadblock." Petra nodded. "I know," she said. It's unlikely."

"You're sure it's her?"

"As sure as I can be."

The snow on the mountains was just visible through the Chinese lanterns and lights bobbing along the side of the road. The wind from the fjord threatened to rip the lightest of the lanterns from their fittings. A raven flapped its wings for balance as it swung back and forth on a dragon's tail wrapped around a streetlight.

"They're amazing," Seabloom said.

"Dragons?"

"Ravens." He pointed at the bird's wingspan, tracing it with a finger in front of him. "It amazes me that they don't go south for the winter." He rested his hand on the door. "It amazes me that you don't."

"This is my home. I can't leave it for six months of the year."

"Six months?"

"Eight, further north."

"Is that where he came from? Maratse?"

Petra turned. "You really do know everything."

"It's my…"

"Job. Yes, I get that. But *everything*?"

"Not everything," Seabloom said. "There are always some blanks, gaps that we have to fill with our best educated guesses."

"You're wrong though," Petra said. "David came from Ittoqqortoormiit, on the east coast."

"But you lived in the north?"

"For a time, yes." Petra took a long, slow breath, almost a whisper. "It was intense – tragic and wonderful at the same time. I want to go back."

"When you retire?"

"How do you…" Petra stopped talking and pressed her lips into a flat smile. *He doesn't know*, she thought. *He's just filling in the blanks.*

The radio display lit up with a burst of chatter at the same time as Seabloom's mobile began to vibrate. He pulled it out of his pocket and turned the screen towards Petra to confirm that Wilkie was in the air and on his way across the fjord.

"ETA thirty seconds," Seabloom said. He pointed at the drone as it twitched in the air above them. The rotors tilted as the drone changed attitude and began to lift into the air. "And we're not the only ones that know. She must be patched into all the channels and frequencies."

"I would bet money on it," Petra said, as she remembered how proficient Ooqi was at intercepting information. Anna Riis had mentioned how Ooqi and Natuk were coding at a young age when they were in her care. "She only has to be half as smart as her brother to run rings around us," she said.

"You don't think she's just half as smart, do you?"

"No, I don't." Petra turned her head to one side as she tried to catch some of the more urgent exchanges on the radio. The officers were talking in Danish – it was faster than communicating in Greenlandic – but the occasional expression slipped through with bursts of excitement. "They've spotted her," Petra said, as she pulled away from the snow-packed curb and accelerated.

The rotor chop of the Coast Guard helicopter shuddered through the air above them, fracturing the shattered edges of the SUV's rear window as Wilkie hovered above Petra and Seabloom. The last of the safety glass clinging to the rubber weather strip fell with a soft tinkle onto the backseat. Petra might have heard it if it wasn't for the chop of the helicopter, the buzz of the drone, and the excited chatter on the radio. Natuk – if it was her – had just bumped the motorbike up the bonnet and over the roof of one of the police cars. Guns had been drawn, but no shots fired.

"Why aren't they shooting?" Seabloom said. "Why won't they stop her?"

"Because it *is* Natuk," Petra said. "They must

have recognised her."

The air stilled as the helicopter flew on towards the roadblock and the drone received a new tasking. Petra watched as it raced towards the roadblock. She imagined that Natuk would programme it to follow the first car to give chase. She almost smiled when the drone locked on to the lead police car. The lights of the Coast Guard helicopter blinked in the sky above the street.

"It's getting dark," Seabloom said.

"*Mitaartut*," Petra said.

"What?"

"Twelfth Night. It starts soon."

"That's January sixth. We've only got the fifth today."

"But if we don't catch her before tomorrow night, there's no telling what she might do."

"Why?"

"Because tomorrow is Natuk's birthday. She was a twin, before I killed her brother. She's also working to an agenda laid out by her foster mother."

"Anna Riis?"

"Yes," Petra said. She stopped herself from asking how he might know that. "We've got her in custody at the detention centre." Petra increased speed, closing the distance between them and the last car in the line of three police cars chasing Natuk.

"I think we need to go pay her a visit," Seabloom said. "With your permission of course."

Petra smiled. "You've provided us with a helicopter, I'm pretty sure I can argue why you should be present at an interview."

"Good," Seabloom said. His mobile vibrated with an incoming call and he answered it, nodding and giving brief commands as Petra increased speed. "She's gone off road," he said.

"I can see that." Petra pointed at the police cars sliding to a stop in a bluster of snow that pillowed around each car. Petra stopped the car and got out. She pointed at the helicopter as Seabloom got out of the passenger side. "There," she said.

"Got it." Seabloom nodded. He rested his mobile on the roof of the car as he tugged on a pair of gloves and a hat. "Talk to me Wilkie," he said, as a cone of glacial light jerked across the slope of snow and granite as the helicopter crew searched for Natuk. "The tracks stop," Seabloom said. "She must be on foot, but they can't see any footprints."

"Then she must be hiding, somewhere close to the bike," Petra said.

Seabloom shook his head. "Wilkie says no. It's pretty flat there. But no tracks."

"What about the rocks?" Petra asked. "Are they black?"

"Some of them." Seabloom pressed his hand to one ear. "More now that Wilkie is hovering lower."

Petra could see drifts of snow curling and swirling, tornado-like, as the Coast Guard helicopter began a slow circle of the area. Natuk had gone to ground between Chinatown and Little Amsterdam. *But where will she go now?*

"There," Seabloom shouted. He pulled the mobile from his ear and pointed, finger extended, at two black shapes running across the closest ridge of rocks, just above the road.

The police raced along the road, hands on their holstered pistols, as they ordered the two fugitives off the ridge. Petra saw hands being raised, and then the lights from the helicopter blinked once as Wilkie flew to a position high above the road. The cone of light lit the two women as they slid down the rocks and into the arms of the police.

"It's not them," Petra said, as they walked towards the police. "Look at their hair."

Petra held her hand to her eyes to shield them from the intense light streaming from the helicopter. The black sheen of the Greenlanders' hair was unmistakeable, as were the masks they wore – replicas of the mask Petra had seen on Viola's face. The two young Greenlanders grinned as Petra approached. They laughed at the look on Seabloom's face until the police officers cuffed them and marched them back to the police cars parked at crazy angles on the side of the road, stepping over one of the masks that fell from the face of the youngest of the two suspects.

Seabloom glanced up at the helicopter, ordering the pilot to do one more sweep as Petra stooped to pick up the mask. She turned it in the light, until the helicopter was gone. The light of day was fading fast. Petra handed the mask to Seabloom.

"What are they usually made of?" he asked.

"Clay and wood," Petra said. "You can get replicas in plaster and plastic.

"But not printed," he said, as he scratched his nail against an anomalous ridge between the holes for the eyes. The rest of the inside of the mask was smooth. "We're going to see more of these," he said.

Chapter 12

Anna Riis caught a glimpse of the waiting room of the detention centre as she was escorted to one of the larger meeting rooms. She remembered that it resembled a mini courtroom, with raised seats curving around the walls on tiers either side of the judge's seat in the middle. There was a platform below it, and a table each for the defendant and the prosecutor. Behind them was a single row for the public, journalists and assorted visitors that Anna had no time for. She wondered if this was it, that her hearing had been bumped up by a matter of hours instead of days, but the mini courtroom was empty but for the two people seated at the table reserved for the prosecution. Anna sneered as she recognised the Commissioner's long black hair, tied haphazardly in a ponytail at the back of her head. The white man beside her was new.

"Hello, Anna," Petra said. She gestured at a third chair at the table. "Will you sit down?"

Anna ignored the man and glared at Petra as the guard removed her cuffs. She looked over her shoulder as the guard left the courtroom and locked the door behind her.

"I suppose I could sit," she said. "You've got a new dog?" Anna said, as she sat down.

"What?"

"Where's your pit bull? The stupid Greenlander with the shotgun?"

"I assume the dog you're referring to is me," Seabloom said. "I'm with the United States Coast Guard, and I have a few questions for you."

"An American?" Anna almost cursed as she

heard the light tone in her voice. It was almost girlish. She adjusted her pitch, switched to English, and said, "What's your interest, Commander?"

"You know my rank?"

"I used to be in politics. I brokered the deal for the Dutch to establish a climate colony south of Nuuk, and I heard enough whispers about the Coast Guard and their interest in a base in Nuuk in the corridors of Christiansborg long before that. Yes, I know your rank, and I know the kind of man who possesses it." Anna glanced at Petra as she said the word *man*.

"Christiansborg?" Seabloom said.

"The Danish Houses of Parliament," Petra said.

"Where the real seat of power is." Anna allowed herself a grin as she turned to face Petra. "Just how long do you think Pipaluk Uutaaq's fledgling government will be able to run this country? How long before they start begging the Chinese or the Americans for money, and help, and then more money?"

"As long as it takes," Petra said.

"Oh, you're a believer now. Is that it?" Anna laughed. "You're just one more Greenlander with a warped sense of independence. And you, a Commissioner. You should know better, Petra Jensen, with your Danish name and your puppet position."

Petra waited a beat as she absorbed the blow. She raised her hand as Seabloom started to speak. "It's alright, let her have her say."

"My say?" Anna spat. "You can't even speak Greenlandic."

"And yet, my name is *Piitalaat*," Petra said, as she

looked at Seabloom. "It's Greenlandic for…"

"Petra," he said. "I've done my homework."

Anna started to clap.

"This is so sweet. You don't need me at all. Why don't I go back to my cell and the two of you can continue this charming little chat without me. Three really is a crowd, as they say." Anna pressed her hands on the table and turned her head to call for the guard.

"I saw Natuk today," Petra said.

Anna felt her body shrink. Her shoulders hunched over the table and her head dipped. The rough weave of the prison cardigan scratched her chin, but it could have been silk for all the reaction it elicited. Anna sighed and then raised her head. She ignored Seabloom and focused on Petra.

"Where?"

"On the bridge across Kangerluarsunnguaq Fjord. And then again as we chased her through Chinatown."

"We thought you might be interested in filling in the blanks," Seabloom said.

"What blanks?"

"Gaps in our information." He stood up and placed the tablet in front of Anna. "This is Natuk, isn't it?"

"Yes."

"This was taken around the time of Ooqi Kleemann's death. What would she be doing on a fishing trawler?"

Anna moved her tongue around her mouth. "Is there any water?"

"I'll get some in a minute," Seabloom said. "Answer the question, Anna."

"Why do you want to know?"

"That's not important right now."

"Of course, it is," Anna said, and laughed. "Why else would you be here?" She looked at Petra. "Why else would the *Commissioner* pay me a visit?"

"Enough."

Anna stopped when Seabloom slammed his hand on the surface of the table. She jerked back in her seat and looked at him.

"Not so different from your pit bull after all, eh, *Piitalaat*."

"Your evasiveness is going to add years to your sentence," Seabloom said.

"Maybe, but you won't get a word out of me about Natuk." Anna looked at Petra. "You took one of my children from me, already. I won't help you take the other one."

Her words hung in the air as the guard unlocked the door and looked inside the room. Seabloom waved her away and Petra nodded. Once the door was locked, it was Petra's turn to talk. She stood up and moved away from the table. Petra leaned against the wood panel separating the first row of tiered seats from the defendant's table.

"Ombudsman Anna Riis was Natuk and Ooqi's foster mother," she said to Seabloom. "She loved them, I don't doubt that, and they could feel it. It was perhaps the first time an adult showed them true love. In Natuk's case it, Anna was the first adult to touch her without leaving a scar – physical or mental." Petra paused at the thought of her own scars, both kinds, and realised that she and Natuk had so many things in common. *Which is probably what makes this so difficult*, she thought.

"You're forgetting something," Anna said. "They

were malnourished. I was the first adult to give them the food they needed. Ooqi, especially, was small for his age."

"You gave them decent clothes, too," Petra said. "And you helped them with their schooling." She looked at Seabloom. "Anna used her own money to supplement the twin's education. She taught them to code."

Seabloom snorted. "Yeah, that makes sense."

"But you had a purpose, Anna," Petra said. "Didn't you?"

Anna caught Petra's eye and then looked away.

"You see," Petra continued, "Anna saw something in those kids, something she could use, if she sowed the right seeds. So, she showed them the very best of what Denmark had to offer, and she compared that with a poisonous image of the country of their birth. She turned them against Greenland."

"But they lived here?" Seabloom said. "They were police officers."

"She put them there," Petra said. "Encouraged them to do well, and to work hard, until she needed them."

"She turned the kids into sleeper agents," Seabloom said. He looked down at Anna. "That's harsh. Your own children."

"Foster children," Anna said. "I gave them a good life."

"And in return, you asked them to give theirs," Petra said. She walked towards the table and stood in front of Anna. "The city is plastered with graffiti. A mask and text in Greenlandic. The text translates into passages from Shakespeare." Petra paused as Anna looked at her. "*Twelfth Night*," she said. "Your favourite play, and the twin's birthday. There's no doubt in my mind that you orchestrated Ooqi's campaign of terror…"

"You can't prove that," Anna said.

"Not yet. But the difference is that this time, you're behind bars, locked away. If Natuk is working to fulfil your agenda, she's doing it alone, Anna."

"She's a clever girl. She doesn't need me."

"That's right. She doesn't," Petra said. "So, what happens when she deviates from your plan? What happens when she takes matters into her own hands? Will you be able to live with Natuk's version of the future you want Greenland to inherit? Have you thought about that?" Petra took a step backwards and waited.

Anna looked over her shoulder at the door.

"The guard isn't coming, Anna," Petra said. "No-one is."

The table creaked as Seabloom stood up. He walked to Petra's side and whispered in her ear. The corners of Anna's eyes creased as she tried to hear what was said. It was about Natuk. *More lies*, she thought. Natuk is a good girl. She will succeed where her brother failed. She was always the smarter of the two. *And that should worry you, Anna*. The voice was her own, inside her head, and it only made Petra's words more convincing.

Natuk unleashed and unchecked. There was no telling what she was capable of.

Anna recalled the Greenlandic play Natuk had written in the style of Shakespeare. She remembered the crudely-drawn figures, and the passionate flecks darting across Natuk's eyes as she explained what happened to whom and why. Natuk always had a *why* as if every action, no matter how small, always had a counter reaction. It was nature's way. It was Natuk's way. The Greenlanders were physically and emotionally closer to nature than most of the people on the Earth. What if Natuk allowed her Greenlandic roots to filter through the years of preparation and conviction Anna had instilled in her? She might be dangerous. She might derail the whole thing.

Anna felt sweat begin to bead on her brow, and a cold hand seemed to clasp her heart. It began to squeeze. She felt faint. Anna started to rise, pressing her hands on the table, but it slid across the floor, and she fell. She felt hands grip and turn her, laying her on her back. Then there was something cool on her lips – a cold glass – and water dribbled into her mouth. She looked up. She reached for Petra with a trembling hand and pinched the sleeves of the Commissioner's jacket between weak fingers. So weak.

"Slowly now, Anna," Petra said.

"You have to…"

"Have to what, Anna?"

"You have to stop her."

"Stop Natuk?"

"Yes," Anna said. "You're right, she's out of control. Out of my control." Anna's voice tapered to a whisper and Petra leaned closer.

"You're going to have to help us," she said

"But she needs to rest first," Seabloom said.

He nodded for the guard to remove the glass of water. And then, when a second guard arrived, he helped Anna to her feet. The guards supported her to the door as Anna shuffled between them. She didn't look back, only forwards, straight ahead and along the corridor. She stopped at the first security door, leaning against the second guard as the first fumbled her keycard from her pocket.

"Allow me."

The voice was gruff, male, Greenlandic. Anna didn't recognise the man, and from the way her guards stiffened, neither did they. A closer look revealed that his prison guard uniform was a little too short; Anna could see a hand's width of his blue shirt between the top of his belt and the bottom of his sweater. His keycard didn't work, and Anna heard him apologise, just a split second before he struck the first guard with his elbow. She sprawled to the floor with blood gushing from her nose. Anna felt a spatter of blood land on her cheeks, and then more as the man used his fist to the same effect on the second guard. Both of them lay sprawled on the floor, as the man gripped Anna by the arm and switched to Danish.

"Anna Riis," he said. "My name is Angut. Natuk sent me."

"Natuk?"

"*Aap*. I'm going to take you to her."

"No," Anna said.

The muscles in Anna's legs jellied. She cried out as Angut lifted her in his arms and carried her over the guards sprawled in the corridor. She heard the sound of the door to the courtroom opening, and then a shout – something in English, an American accent. And then Angut started to run, pressing Anna's nose into the smoky wool of his tight-fitting sweater. She could hardly breathe, as he clamped her body to his and kicked, punched and elbowed his way through the outer layer of security. Anna heard him grunt several times, recognising a single word here and there, often in the pause at a secure door, as he waited for someone to open it.

Not someone, she realised. *It was Natuk.*

Chapter 13

They waited inside the hollow beneath the boulder until the helicopter had returned to the Coast Guard base and the police had left with the two suspects in custody. The snow filled the tread of their boots and plastered their overtrousers as Natuk led Viola between boulders of granite above the dragon-lit streets of Chinatown. The mining town was a bitter pill for many Greenlanders to swallow. Natuk remembered the initial argument to build the town for the Chinese miners needed for the mine located in the very north of Nuuk fjord. The original plans located the town close to the mine, but it proved easier to house the miners at the mine, and their families and the families of the additional workers closer to the city of Nuuk. The arrival of three thousand new residents with a variety of ailments not shared by the Greenlanders threatened to overwhelm the existing hospital and medical services. The announcement and building of Kong Frederik's Hospital, a very modern and sophisticated institution, made the lack of mining jobs for Greenlanders a little more palatable. Greenland was used to buying in or trading for foreign expertise, but the initial excitement surrounding the promise of *some* jobs for the locals proved to be nothing more than noise and political bluster. A couple of cleaning jobs and the obligatory translator position was the extent of the Greenlandic roster of workers at the Chinese mine. Natuk paused to look down at the pretty lights and dragons and tried to remember her foster mother's comments when the deal had been struck – something about *ignorant enthusiasm* and *nothing new.*

"Greenland," Anna Riis had said, "just isn't ready to make deals on this scale."

The Greenland Self Rule government had argued for the right to negotiate their own terms, and Denmark had agreed. When plans for the Kong Frederik's Hospital had been leaked, Anna had scoffed, encouraging Natuk and her brother to look closely, and not be distracted by the political smokescreen.

"It's like *Twelfth Night*," she said. "A flattering letter left in the right place to be found at the right time. You can be sure that Denmark has negotiated that on behalf of the Greenland government, and the so-called leak has been seized by that upstart Malik Uutaaq. But," Anna said over dinner that night, "credit where credit is due, he handled the leak masterfully, and now the people are placated, once again, revelling in the shrewdness of their politicians, once again."

But for how long? Natuk wondered, as she slipped her glasses into the inside pocket of her jacket. Greenland couldn't be ruled by a government that profited from opportunists. When Denmark retreated, and the real playmakers and dealmakers were gone, what then? How long would it take before Greenland was railroaded by a more mature government from a country with a history of colonisation and manipulation? Perhaps even more chequered than the Danes?

Natuk stopped as Viola stumbled over a stretch of ice-filmed boulders. She took her hand and guided her to the deeper snow on the other side.

"Are you alright?" she asked.

"Cold," Viola said.

Natuk pressed her hands against Viola's cheeks and brushed clumps of snow from her hair. She kissed her nose, nibbled at her lips, slipping her tongue briefly between them.

"Your hands are so warm," Viola said, as Natuk brushed at another clump of snow. "How can that be? You have no gloves."

"You know what they say," Natuk said. "Warm hands, cold heart." The light of the late afternoon moon lit her teeth and turned her blonde hair white.

Viola took her hand. "I don't believe that."

Natuk kissed her and tugged at her hand. "We have to keep moving. There's a car waiting for us."

Natuk led the way, breaking a trail through the deep snow and the deeper drifts. It was wetter and denser than the snow she remembered from the north of Greenland, when she and Ooqi had lived in Upernavik with relations. The snow on the mountains around Nuuk required more effort, pumping more blood around her body as she pushed forwards, it kept her hands warm. She smiled at the thought, but her lips flattened when she saw the lights of Little Amsterdam ahead of them.

The lights reminded her that her foster mother wasn't always right. In fact, there were times when Natuk had questioned her reasoning. There had been arguments. Anna blamed it on Natuk's teenage temper, tossing her comments and political naivety to one side – chaff to be discarded and ignored.

"One day you will understand," Anna had said when the initial ideas for the Dutch climate colony in Greenland had been discussed.

They were still in Denmark at the time, and Natuk remembered slamming the front door of the house, and the bewildered look in Ooqi's eyes. He always had been more impressionable. Anna's favourite.

"And now he is dead," she said, as she stopped at the top of the slope leading down to the road. The streets of Little Amsterdam were littered with artificial trees. Draped in strings of white lights, they glittered beneath the black winter sky.

"Are you alright?" Viola asked. She took Natuk's hand.

"You did well at the bridge," Natuk said.

"I did?"

Natuk turned to look at Viola. "You showed your face. You rallied people."

"I was wearing a mask," Viola said, tapping the cargo pocket of her jacket.

"It's not a mask anymore, Viola, it's a symbol. *You* are a symbol." She pressed her hands around Viola's shoulders, turning her south to look at Chinatown. "Greenland has made some poor decisions since you were born. Decisions that you and your children have to live with." Natuk turned Viola to the north to face Little Amsterdam. "Some of the decisions were made for Greenland, supposedly in Greenland's favour. There are some people who would argue that Greenland is not mature enough to make its own decisions."

"That's what you believe?"

Natuk shook her head. "Not exactly. But it's what I was brought up to believe. My brother died for that belief." Natuk paused. She slipped her hands down Viola's arms and pressed her fingers into Viola's gloved palms. "I loved my brother. I always will. He was convinced that the people of Greenland need someone strong to guide them."

"But you don't?"

"I did once, but not anymore."

"Then what do you believe?"

Natuk looked up as thick clumps of snow started to fall, plastering Viola's head and clinging to her hair.

"I believe we need to make a change. We can't trust the governments of Greenland or Denmark to make decisions for us – we will have to live with those decisions long after they are dead and gone. It's time for us to make a difference. If Greenland is going to be independent, if we are to be the youngest government in the world, then the young need to lead it. We're going to need a leader," she said. "Someone to follow." Natuk gripped Viola's hands. "*You.*"

"Me?"

Viola shivered. She stumbled backwards, but Natuk caught her.

"You led the people on the bridge."

"I was excited by the crowd. I didn't know what I was doing."

"They followed you anyway."

Viola shook her head. "I don't know…"

"You made the First Minister stumble at the press conference."

"Only because I asked *your* question."

"I wasn't there, Viola. It was you. You asked the question." Natuk pulled Viola close, pressed her forehead against Viola's and caressed her cheek. "Greenland's youth needs a leader. They will follow you."

"But why me? Why can't they follow you?"

"*Naamik*," Natuk said. "I'm not a leader. I work better behind the scenes."

"Pulling the strings?" Viola shivered again, stronger this time, "Are you pulling my strings? Are you manipulating me?"

Natuk pressed her cheek against Viola's. She nibbled at her ear, melting snowflakes with her warm breath as she whispered, "You are not a puppet, Viola. You are the future."

"I'm scared," she said.

"Of what?"

"Of leading people," Viola pulled away from Natuk. "Those two girls, the ones the police arrested. One of them was pretending to be me. And now she is in trouble."

"She's not in trouble," Natuk said. "The police will let her go – they'll let both of them go – as soon as they have asked them a few questions."

"How do you know?"

"Because I used to be a police officer," Natuk said. She frowned for a second. "I suppose I still am."

"But they sacrificed themselves to protect us…"

"Sacrifice is a strong word, Viola."

"And you keep calling me *Viola*. Stop that. You have to stop." Viola wrenched free of Natuk's hands and stepped backwards onto a crust of snow. "I'm not who you think I am. I'm not even who you want me to be. I can't be that person. I don't want to lead people. I don't want to run the country."

Natuk laughed. "You're sweet when you're upset," she said. Natuk held out her arms. "Viola, please."

"I don't know," Viola said. She stamped her foot and sank into the snow to her knee. She leaned to one side, wobbled for a second, and then fell, driving her arms deep into the snow as she tried to stop her fall.

Natuk giggled.

"Stop it," Viola said.

"You're even sweeter now."

"Stop laughing and help me." Viola rolled onto her side and pulled one arm free. "Natuk."

Natuk took a step forwards, spread her weight evenly, and took another step towards Viola. She gripped her by the arm and slowly pulled her out of the snow and onto her feet. Natuk led Viola onto the top of a flat boulder. She brushed the snow from her back and sides. When she was done, Natuk reached forwards and tucked a strand of Viola's hair behind her ear.

"You don't have to run the country, Viola," she said. "You just have to inspire people."

"I can't do that."

"It's too late," Natuk said. "You've already begun."

Natuk reached inside her jacket and tugged her glasses out of her pocket. She slipped them onto her face and checked the battery icon. The short time she had kept the glasses close to her body had been enough to preserve the battery long enough to check the status of the drones and to confirm that a car had been sent to pick them up.

"They're waiting for us," she said, and took Viola's hand.

"How do you pay for all this?"

"I don't. All the technology is paid for from a fund set up many years ago."

"What fund?" Viola stumbled over a boulder and leaned against Natuk.

"Someone has been preparing for this day for a long time."

"Who?"

"You'll meet her, soon," Natuk said. She pointed at the road below them. "There's our car."

Natuk didn't say another word until they were sat on the back seat. The driver, one of the young Greenlanders who had assembled and steered the drones from the abandoned store in Nuuk, turned up the heat and drove through Little Amsterdam towards Nuuk. Natuk scrolled through the DataStream in her glasses. She opened an encrypted message with a blink, holding her eye open for a retinal scan. Her hand shook as she read the message from Angut.

"What's wrong?" Viola asked.

"Nothing."

"Your hand is shaking." Viola squeezed Natuk's fingers. "And it's cold."

"I'm fine."

Viola laughed. "A minute ago, on the mountain, you were comforting me. It was me that needed reassuring."

Natuk shrugged. "I'm fine." She closed the message and slipped her glasses into her pocket. "We'll be there soon, and I'll tell you what happens next."

Natuk looked out of the window and thought about Angut's message. Anna Riis was free. He would take her to the fishing trawler, as agreed. But it was his last comment that worried Natuk.

She knows.

Two words, but enough for Natuk to lose control, if only for a second. Viola had felt it. *It can't happen again*, she thought.

"What's next?" Viola asked, as the driver looped around the block to check they weren't being followed, before backing into the alleyway at the rear of the store.

"*Next* is *mitaartut*," Natuk said. "Twelfth Night." She smoothed her hand through Viola's hair. "January 6th is also my birthday. There's going to be a party, and all of Greenland is invited."

Chapter 14

Pipaluk put her mobile on mute and hid it beneath the towels she had piled on the toilet seat. She slipped into the bath, wincing as the water scalded her skin. She held onto the sides, slipped her legs all the way into the tub and felt the water melt the outer layers of her skin as she lay down. It was too early for a bath. There were a hundred things she had to do, but since the first reports came in of the disturbance on the bridge, and when the police bustled outside her door and her security was downgraded from the leader of the SRU to a Constable, Pipaluk decided nothing really mattered anymore, at least not for the next hour, an hour she planned to enjoy.

As the bath bubbles popped and the water singed her exposed knees, breasts and neck, Pipaluk remembered her father's belief that Greenland had to stay primitive in order to appeal to the tourists. He worked hard to promote the image of the Greenlanders before they were *civilised*, encouraging the building of sod and turf houses on historical sites within an hour's journey by boat of each of the main towns and villages. He encouraged the tourist companies to populate the fake settlements each summer with traditionally clad *natives*, funding the projects with government support. When the tourists asked if people really lived like that in modern Greenland, the guides were instructed to be ambiguous. Pipaluk worked as a guide in one of the settlements one summer, and soon discovered that the more ambiguous she was, the greater the tip. The bathwater rippled, and the bubbles popped as she smiled at the memory of spending that summer's earnings on designer clothes and make-up.

Anything for the money, she thought, as she moved her legs.

The thought soured her luxurious mood, and Pipaluk tried to flush it away with more hot water. She turned the taps with her toes, cursing at the hot metal faucet that burned her skin. It wasn't the only thing that burned. The demonstrators, and that *girl's* insinuations that Pipaluk was hiding something, that she had ulterior motives and designs for an independent Greenland. *How dare she*, she thought. *She has no idea how hard I have worked for this*. The Calendar Man and his campaign of terror had nearly been the end of Pipaluk's term as First Minister, *and nearly the end of an independent Greenland*, she thought. But the dream of independence survived. It gathered even more support, and grew stronger, bigger, and more realistic. *Until today.*

Pipaluk turned the tap and stopped the flow of water. She bent her legs and slipped under the water, pressing her fingers to the sides of the bath as she slid deeper into the tub.

She didn't hear the first vibrations of an incoming message, and she didn't check either. Pipaluk waited until the water began to cool and her skin changed colour from lava red to European white. She felt goose bumps prickle her skin and had to rub the colour back into her legs, her stomach and her arms with the towel. She glimpsed the first message on the screen of her mobile as it fell onto the floor.

Pipaluk let the towel fall and bent down to pick up her mobile. Her wet hair clung to her cheeks, damp and slightly cold. She brushed it behind her ear as she read the first message – an update from the bridge.

The second message was more interesting. Juuarsi had been contacted by someone who knew the girl responsible for inciting the young Greenlanders to act, at the press conference and later, on the bridge.

His next message encouraged Pipaluk to dry herself and dress quickly. Juuarsi had brought the contact to the hotel, and they were waiting for her in the Skyline bar.

Pipaluk pulled a pair of jeans over her panties, stuffed her feet into thick socks and pulled on a pair of sealskin boots. She left the boot zips open halfway. She found a thick cotton shirt and buttoned it over her bare chest. She stuffed her mobile in her back pocket and pulled on a black sealskin gilet. She smiled at her reflection in the mirror as she fixed her hair with a patterned headband. If it wasn't for the years, she might have been looking at a younger version of herself, ready to take on the world, and the tourists.

"The world first," she said, as she grabbed the keycard for the suite. "The tourists can wait."

There was no telling what Juuarsi's source might reveal about Tiina Markussen – the so-called *Viola*. But the potential to change the status quo and for damage control buoyed Pipaluk along the corridor; the Constable guarding her had to jog to keep up.

She paused at the entrance to the bar, spotted Juuarsi as he raised his hand to wave to her and walked to his table. Pipaluk checked the frown she felt wrinkling her forehead beneath her headband when she saw the man sitting next to Juuarsi. He looked like one of the demonstrators she had seen at the press conference. He could easily have been one of the people jostling her car or thumping on the windows. She decided there wasn't much that she liked about his appearance, or his behaviour. He cast furtive glances around Pipaluk, barely registering her as he scanned the bar. She almost turned her head to see what he was so afraid of. When he did look at her, Pipaluk forced a smile and sat down. She waved the Constable away to a nearby table and nodded when Juuarsi asked if he should order more drinks.

"The usual," Pipaluk said, as Juuarsi caught the eye of the waiter.

"This is the man I told you about," Juuarsi said, once the waiter had gone.

"What's your name?" Pipaluk asked.

"No names," the man said.

He tilted his head to one side and looked around Pipaluk. The frown hidden beneath Pipaluk's headband deepened, pinching the skin around her eyes as she looked at her assistant.

"Perhaps you can tell the First Minister what you told me," he said.

"About her?" the man said.

"Yes."

The man paused as the waiter returned with their drinks, and then leaned over the table, beckoning for Pipaluk to lean closer.

"She's well organised," he said. "And a real bitch. If she saw me with you, or with them." He nodded at the police Constable. "She'd gut me. I'm sure of it."

"Gut you?" Pipaluk struggled at the thought of Viola carrying a knife, let alone sticking it into the stomach of the man sitting opposite her.

"*Aap*," he said. "That's right."

"Tell her about the drones," Juuarsi said.

"There's lots of them. We built them not far

from here."

"Drones?"

"Expensive ones. They've got four or five cameras on each one."

Pipaluk leaned back in her seat. She studied the man as he scanned the bar once more. He was about the same age as Viola. He dressed like a student, but his eyes lacked something – there was no spark to them, just a dull glow that pulsed with tension.

"I don't understand," Pipaluk said. "What are you talking about?"

"Your assistant said you wanted to know about the girl."

"I do."

"I know all about her. I know where she is, where the drones are." He paused to lower his voice. "I even know what she plans to do."

"And what's that?"

"*Mitaartut*," he said.

"That's tomorrow night," Pipaluk said. "What about it?"

"That's when she's going to strike."

"Viola?"

"Who?" It was the man's turn to frown.

"You said Viola is going to strike tomorrow night."

"I don't know anyone called Viola."

"Then who are you talking about?"

"The girl. The woman with the blonde hair and the black eyebrows. She's going to cause a riot. She's going to get everyone to march on the streets with masks and sticks, just like you do on *mitaartut*, but everyone."

"Juuarsi," Pipaluk said. "I honestly don't know

what this man is talking about." She stood up to leave. "I think it's best if you take him to the police. He can tell them all about it."

"No," the man said. "I can't talk to the police. She *is* the police. She'll know. Then she'll find me and kill me."

"Pipaluk," Juuarsi said. "I think this is important. It must be connected with the graffiti."

"It is," the man said.

"Fine." Pipaluk sat down. "But I want to know your name before I hear another word. I won't act on the words of a stranger."

The man glanced around the room for the fourth time since she had arrived. He took a breath. "My name is Qallu," he said.

"And your surname?"

"Just Qallu."

"Okay," Pipaluk said. "The blonde woman you described, the one who's not Viola."

"*Aap.*"

"You say she's a policewoman?"

"I think she used to be."

Pipaluk looked at her assistant. She beckoned for him to lean closer and whispered in his ear, "I think he means Natuk Petersen."

"I think so too."

"You told me he knew Viola."

"I was mistaken," Juuarsi said. "But maybe this is even more important? Unless they're connected?"

"They're definitely connected," Pipaluk said.

Pipaluk took a sip of her wine, watching Qallu over the lip of her glass. It was coming back to her now. The woman Qallu described, the woman he was so clearly frightened of, was one of Petra's own officers, gone rogue, and determined to destroy everything Pipaluk had achieved so far. He knew where she was, but it seemed unlikely that she would still be there. Unless, of course, she didn't know he was here.

"How did you get away, Qallu? Did you just walk away or sneak out the back?"

"What?"

"You said you know where she is, this woman. I think you're talking about Natuk Petersen, and if it *is* her, then I really need you to tell me where she is. I can send people there to get her, and we can protect you."

"You can't protect me," he said. "She has eyes everywhere."

"They why did you come to me?" Juuarsi said.

"I want a plane ticket to Denmark."

"There are no flights today," Juuarsi said.

"I want to be on the first flight tomorrow. When I'm on the plane, I'll send you a text with her location. Not before."

"You said she was planning something for *mitaartut*," Pipaluk said. "That's tomorrow. We need to act now."

"It's tomorrow *night*," Qallu said. "I'll tell you where she is when I am on the plane."

And she'll be long gone, Pipaluk thought. She took another sip of wine and looked around the bar as Qallu scanned the patrons for a fifth time. *He feels safer here*, she thought. *Why?* Pipaluk looked at the couple at the table nearest them. They were in their late thirties, the same as her. The two men drinking at the bar, judging by the size of their guts and their jowls, were closer to fifty, maybe older. The other patrons were aged somewhere in-between. They had the money to drink in the hotel bar, or their employer was paying for the room and the drinks. This was a different crowd to the one Qallu was a part of, different in age and intensity. *That's why he feels safe here.* Pipaluk finished her wine.

"Juuarsi will get you a room for the night. I want you to stay in it."

"And the flight?"

"We'll pay for your ticket, but you will tell us where she is tomorrow morning, at breakfast." Pipaluk held up her hand as Qallu opened his mouth to speak. "No exceptions. Your other option is to leave now and take your chances on the street." She stood up. "It's up to you."

Qallu glanced at Juuarsi and nodded. "I'll take the room," he said.

"Good." Pipaluk turned to Juuarsi. "Call the Commissioner. Arrange a breakfast meeting in my suite." Pipaluk paused as she remembered how Petra had reacted in the presence of the American. "Tell her to bring the Coast Guard Commander."

Pipaluk nodded for the Constable to follow her as she passed his table. He didn't have to jog to catch up, but he lengthened his stride to match Pipaluk's. The long soak in the bath had been relaxing, but there was nothing like a shift in the balance of power to rejuvenate Greenland's First Minister. *Viola can wait,* she thought, as she entered her suite. *There are bigger fish in the ocean, and once they are caught, we are back on track.* She stopped in front of the mirror as she removed her gilet. She recognised the same smile from her youth. It was her father's smile, the one that creased his lips when he dreamed of an independent

Greenland.

"I'm going to make it happen, *ata*," Pipaluk said. "I'm not going to let anyone get in the way of a free and independent Greenland. Not a silly girl and certainly not some crooked cop."

Pipaluk removed her headband, smoothed her fingers through her hair, and fixed herself a celebratory drink. She turned off the lights and sat at the table by the window as the Northern Lights drifted over her city.

Chapter 15

Petra listened as the Governor explained for the third time that he *couldn't* explain how someone had hacked the detention centre's security system. Nor did he have an explanation as to how someone could overpower a guard and change into their uniform just a few minutes before walking through the front gate and past security without being caught on camera.

"It's a glitch," he said.

"You were hacked," Petra said.

"With respect, Commissioner," the Governor said, "you don't know that for sure."

Petra held up her hands as the Governor opened his mouth to say more. "Please," she said, "let's move on. Just tell me you have at least one image of the man."

"We've got nothing," the Governor said. "The glitch affected all…"

Petra walked away. She waited for the guard to buzz her through the security door, and then joined Seabloom outside. There was a layer of rime ice on the thick collar of his coat where his breath had frozen to the edges. Tiny pearls of ice beaded in the rough wool of the lapels of his jacket, and smaller beads clung to the stubble on his cheeks. Petra chided herself for noticing.

It's alright, Piitalaat.

"No, it's not alright, David. It's too soon."

"What's that?" Seabloom asked, as he pulled his mobile away from his ear.

"What?"

"You said it was too soon."

"I was talking to myself," Petra said. "Have you

found anything?"

"A trail of sorts," Seabloom said. He pointed at a single thick tread pressed into the snow. It snaked up the road towards the runway. "Another motorbike," he said. "It will be long gone by now. And by the time the helicopter gets here, any heat signature will be invisible, just like when we lost your Constable."

Petra nodded. She didn't like to be reminded of losing Natuk. The two youths they had arrested knew just enough to tease the police and nothing more. The message on her phone from Atii revealed they had been released less than an hour after being taken to the police station.

A swirl of blue emergency lights swathed across the snow. Petra heard the siren next and ran through a series of actions in her head as she waited for the two police SUVs to slow to a stop in front of her and Seabloom. Atii was the first out of the vehicle, followed by Aron.

"I had no-one else, ma'am," Atii said, as Petra started to frown. "You wouldn't believe how many officers have called in sick today. Three of them right after they were finished on the bridge. Tavik is losing it."

"Alright," Petra said. She smiled at Aron. "I need you to have a word with the Governor, Aron."

"Yes, ma'am." Aron glanced at the entrance to the detention centre.

"He's going to tell you it was a glitch that allowed someone to walk into the centre and to break out with Anna Riis. But even I know that's not the case. I want you to find out how and who, if you can."

"I thought…" Aron stopped speaking and looked at Atii.

"There is a high chance it was Natuk," Petra said. "But we left her on the side of a mountain somewhere between Chinatown and Little Amsterdam. She's either constantly online or someone else is helping her. I want you to find out."

Petra pulled Atii to one side as Aron walked towards the detention centre. Seabloom followed him, clapping his hands together and brushing the layer of ice from the front of his coat.

"I realise we're short staffed," Petra said, "but what resources do you have here and now?"

"With me?"

"Yes."

"Aron's inside, that leaves me and two officers."

"That's not enough to find Anna Riis."

"*Naamik*," Atii said. "Not nearly enough. We have the regular patrols out, but with two protests in one day, we are feeling it. Everyone's tired. Just one more demonstration will push us to breaking point." She nodded at the detention centre. "What about the Americans?"

"I think that's what Joshua – the Commander – is trying to negotiate," Petra said. "He exhausted the goodwill funds when he ordered the helicopter to assist in the search. I'm not sure he can help us." Petra pressed her hand on Atii's arm. "Sergeant," she said, "Why are you laughing?"

"Sorry, ma'am," Atii said. "I'm not laughing at the situation. It's just…" Atii grinned.

"Come on, Atii. Tell me," Petra said. "At least stop laughing."

Atii shrugged as a civilian car sped into the parking area and skidded to a stop just a few metres from where they stood.

"I tried to stop him," Atii said. "But you know Gaba…"

Yes, Petra thought. *I know Gaba.*

She watched as Gaba Alatak opened the car door and climbed out from behind the steering wheel. He stood up, smoothed a bare hand over his bald head and walked towards them. Atii pushed him away as he tried to kiss her.

"I can't kiss my wife?" he said.

"Right now, I'm a Sergeant on duty. You can kiss me later," she said. "If you've cleaned up after yourself."

"The boys and I got a new toy for Christmas," Gaba said, as he kissed Petra on the cheek. "Atii thinks outboard motors belong on boats, not kitchen tables."

"I'm not having this discussion," Atii said.

She turned to leave.

"Sergeant?" Petra said.

"I'm going to coordinate the search. I'll call Tavik and see who he can spare. Besides," she said, and looked at Gaba, "I think the fewer people that hear your conversation, the better."

Gaba grinned as he watched his wife walk away.

"What's she talking about, Gaba?"

"I have a proposal."

"No," Petra said. "You are under investigation for your role in Ooqi's death. I'm still waiting for the inquiry to reach a decision about my role, and how responsible I am for involving you. If it wasn't for the circumstances surrounding the Calendar Man, I would be suspended, already. I can't have you anywhere near any police investigation, Gaba. Not now, and not in the future, either."

Gaba waited until Petra was finished. He hitched his thumbs into his belt as if he was still wearing a utility belt like the one he wore as leader of Greenland's SRU, the same position his wife now held. Petra sighed as he looked down at her. She consoled herself with the thought that it wasn't personal, Gaba Alatak looked down on everybody. She couldn't even remember a Dane who was as tall as he was. He was a Greenlandic anomaly, and a very old friend.

"Petra," he said. "Do you know how much Âmo Security earned in December?"

"No."

"Enough to give the entire team a Christmas bonus, even the junior members of the team. The Calendar Man might have been bad for Nuuk, but he was good for business. The First Minister paid for two months in advance. But when the threat level dropped, I gave half the team a week's paid leave on the condition that they stay in Nuuk, ready to respond if I need them. That's twenty of my best men and women."

"I'm pleased for you, Gaba, but this is not the time to discuss business." Petra pointed at the detention centre. "I've got an escaped suspect and her crazy foster daughter to find, and…"

"A police department that is overworked, underpaid, and on the edge," Gaba said. "I know. That's why you need my help."

"I can't."

"Off the books."

"What?"

"This is an exceptional situation, Petra. You don't have the resources to get the job done. I'm offering you my help."

"I don't have the resources to hire Âmo either, Gaba."

"I don't mean my company. I mean me."

Petra pressed her hands to her temples.

"Gaba," she said. "I thought I just told you that I couldn't have you anywhere near an official police investigation. What part don't you understand?"

"The *official* part," he said.

Gaba waved as Atii shouted that she was leaving. He waited until her police car had left the parking area and then shrugged.

"I'm bored, Petra," he said. "Running a business is one thing, but I miss the action. The blue lights."

"You're as bad as David," she said.

"Then I'm in good company." Gaba reached out to pull a length of Petra's hair stuck to the corner of her mouth. "Whatever you need done, I'll get it done."

"By the book?"

"Don't ask that, Petra. Just tell me what you need." Gaba glanced at the detention centre as the door opened and a tall man walked towards them. "Just tell me quickly," he said.

Petra glanced over her shoulder as Seabloom approached. She took Gaba's hand, and said, "Find Anna Riis." She let go as soon as Seabloom reached them.

She waited as the two men bristled for a moment. It reminded her of David's sledge dogs. The snow where he kept them was stained with the daily pissing of the Alpha dog's territory, followed by the more physical display of dominance that followed any discretion or opportunity to test the Alpha's ability to lead. It was the same with men and women, but men were less subtle about it. In some ways that made it easier, but Petra didn't have time for two men in their fifties to display their Alpha potential.

"Commander Seabloom," she said, short-circuiting the canine formalities, "this is Gaba Alatak. He used to be leader of the Special Response Unit." Petra waited as the two men shook hands. "He's married to Atii," she added.

Petra couldn't decide if she should read anything into Seabloom's sudden relaxed attitude, or just enjoy the peeved expression on Gaba's face. *Either way*, she thought, *we just don't have time for this.*

"I'll leave you to it," Gaba said. He kissed Petra on the cheek. He waved as he walked to his car.

What have I done? Petra wondered, as Gaba drove away.

"You worked together, I presume," Seabloom said.

"Yes."

"For quite a while?"

"Yes. A long time."

"I don't know how you do it."

"It wasn't easy," Petra said. She smiled at the thought, and the memory of how arrogant and frustrating Gaba could be. It didn't matter if he was an ex-lover, colleague or friend, he would always be *Gaba*.

"I meant, I don't know how you can stand out in the cold so long," Seabloom said. "I'm freezing. Again."

"I'm sorry. I didn't think about it. We can go back inside."

"No," he said. "I have to get back to the base."

Seabloom looked up as it started snowing. "Whatever happened to it being too cold to snow?"

"This is Greenland," Petra said, and smiled.

"It is, and I'm sorry to say that my government is not quite ready to provide any more assistance. Not for the time being. That's why I need to get back, to see if I can move a little money within the budget."

"You don't have to do that."

"Commissioner," he said. "I think we both know that you can use all the help you can get."

"You're right," Petra said. She looked at the road and watched the taillights of Gaba's car disappear around the bend. When they were gone, she started walking back to the detention centre. "I do appreciate all you have done already. I will be grateful for any extra assistance."

"That sounds pretty damned formal, Commissioner. Did I miss something?"

"I don't think so," Petra said, and frowned.

She stopped by her car. The snow fell through the shattered rear window, layering the back seat with a blanket of thick flakes.

"Can I drive you back to the base?"

"I've got a car on the way," Seabloom said. He scratched a clump of snow from his cheek. "I'm sorry, Petra, I'm not very good at this."

"At what?"

"Nothing," he said. "Don't think about it." Seabloom pointed at a large American SUV as it rumbled into the parking area. "That's my ride." He walked to the car and opened the door. "I'll call you as soon as I know more," he said.

"I appreciate it."

I like him, Piitalaat.

"Not now, David. It's not a good time."

Petra's mobile rang as she walked to the entrance of the detention centre. She recognised the number of the First Minister's assistant and sighed. *It's never a good time*, she thought as she answered the call.

Chapter 16

Viola waited in the car in the alleyway as Natuk slipped through the back door of the store. The driver glanced at her a few times in the mirror but said nothing. He smelled of cigarettes and Viola covered her nose with her jacket sleeve. The driver looked at her again, staring this time. Viola turned her head. She could just see the back door.

"She'll be a while," the driver said.

"What?" Viola moved her hand from her nose to her lap.

"Your friend. The blonde."

"Oh."

The seat creaked as the driver turned around to look at her. His hand was just a few inches from Viola's knee. He flicked his finger and it caught the hem of her jacket.

"You're her, aren't you?"

"Who?" Viola said. She shivered as he plucked the jacket between his fingers.

"The girl. The one who's meant to inspire us." The driver grinned, flicking his tongue between brown gums and yellow teeth. "We could get to know each other while she's gone," he said.

He tugged one more time at Viola's jacket, laughing as she twitched. The movement lifted her jacket and exposed her knee. The weave of her overtrousers was coarse and the material was thick, but Viola could feel his fingers burning circles on her skin.

"Stop," she said.

"Why?"

"Because I don't like it."

The driver reached between the car seats and pressed his hand between Viola's knees. She twisted away, and he reached further, grinning as he pawed at her. A sudden rap on the window made him stop, and he pulled his arm away from Viola's legs, twisting in his seat as the passenger door opened.

"Did I scare you?" Natuk asked as she sat on the backseat and closed the door.

Viola stared straight ahead. She caught the driver's look in the mirror, and the tiny shake of his head.

"Viola?" Natuk said. "What's wrong?" Natuk grasped Viola's fingers, squeezing them once to get her attention. "Hey? You there?"

"Yes," Viola whispered. She turned her head and looked at Natuk. She tried to smile. "I'm here."

"You must have been colder than I thought," Natuk said. "We've got one more stop, and then I'll take you somewhere you can rest before *mitaartut*. There won't be any time once we start." Natuk pressed her hand against Viola's cheek. "Hey, relax. You're going to be a star." Natuk looked at the driver. "Take us to the den. You know where."

"*Aap.*"

When Natuk looked away the driver winked at Viola and then started the car. He pulled away from the store and drifted down the alleyway. Natuk leaned back in the seat and put her glasses on. She held Viola's hand as she blinked her way through the DataStream. Viola looked out of the window. She could feel the heat of the driver's look, the intensity of his gaze, but so long as she could also feel Natuk's fingers, slender and strong, she felt safe.

They drove for ten minutes, turning through a

series of narrow snow-lined streets until the driver stopped beside a low wooden house shaped like a long letter L. The roof closest to the street sagged with a winter's worth of wind-blown snow.

"I'll be a few minutes," Natuk said.

Viola caught the driver's eye in the mirror, as Natuk started to open the door. She gripped Natuk's hand and moved to follow her.

"I'll come with you," she said.

"I'm not so sure. It's not exactly the nicest of places."

"I don't mind. I'll come anyway."

Viola opened her door as Natuk hesitated. She zipped her jacket to her chin as Natuk walked around the car to join her.

"You won't have seen anything like this before," Natuk said.

"I'll be okay."

"If you're sure." Natuk plucked at a length of Viola's hair that was caught in her jacket zip. "Okay, but I need you to wait while I talk to someone inside. He's got some information I need. Something he doesn't want to share in the DataStream." She took her glasses off and slipped them into her jacket pocket.

Natuk led Viola to the front door. It was jammed open with a drift of snow. She pushed it open and tugged Viola by the hand, leading her through the doorway and into a cold room with black plastic taped to the windows and a thin crust of ice on the walls. There was snow on the floor, and a broken wooden pallet with half a rusted oil drum positioned in the middle of it. A low flame licked at the solid fuel bricks inside it. Natuk pointed at the sofa and the woman bent over the arm at one end. Viola frowned at the rattling sound the woman was making as she breathed.

"You can wait there," Natuk said. "She won't bother you."

Viola nodded and picked her way across the floor, weaving between a litter of bottles and food wrappers. The woman's wheeze deepened, and the rattle in her lungs became a click like a set of rusty cogs as Viola sat down at the other end of the sofa. Natuk waited for Viola to nod before pointing at a door at the end of a long corridor.

"I'll be ten minutes," she said.

Viola watched her walk down the corridor and enter the far room. Natuk closed the door behind her leaving Viola sitting in the gloom with dirty snow and a woman with rattle lung for company.

The driver entered the room half a minute later.

Viola stiffened at the sound of the front door scraping over the drift of packed snow. The smell of his cigarettes seeped into the room ahead of him, followed by his shadow, his sneer, and the dull glint of the knife in his hand.

"I thought we could finish what we started," he said, as he walked across the room. He moved quickly, pressing his hand on Viola's shoulder as she tried to stand, and the blade at her throat as she opened her mouth to scream. "Not a word," he said. "Or I'll cut you."

The blade scraped up and down Viola's skin as she trembled, half standing, her knees bent, fingers stiff and useless at her sides.

"Now," the driver said, "unzip your trousers." He looked over his shoulder, staring at the door at the end of the corridor for a second, before stepping closer to Viola. "Faster," he said, as she fumbled with the zip of her jacket.

The driver's breathing changed to a kind of huffing, bestial, like a bear, as he unsnapped his jeans and reached inside his pants. Viola choked on the draught of stale cigarette smoke that he breathed in her face. She felt tears well in her eyes, and then she gasped, choking on a sob as the driver grew tired of waiting and gripped a fistful of her trousers and tugged them down her legs.

It was the last thing he did.

Viola didn't see or hear Natuk enter the room, but she felt the brush of air on her face and across her thighs as the driver toppled onto his side. The tip of the knife nicked the hem of her jacket, catching in the stitches for a second until the driver jerked it free and slashed at the air in front of Viola.

"Idiot," Natuk said, as she bent the driver's wrist until he dropped the knife.

He kicked out at her, and then cursed as Natuk curled the toe of her boots into his knee. He cursed her again as she pressed the muzzle of her pistol into his cheek.

"Hey, no mess."

Natuk paused to glance at the man who entered the room. She nodded at the litter on the floor.

"Mess?"

"Body fluids then," the man said. "Take it outside."

"You hear that?" Natuk said, as she pressed the muzzle deeper into the driver's cheek. "I've got to take the trash out."

"Police bitch," the driver said.

"You're half right," she said, and gripped the driver's jacket.

Natuk pulled the driver to his feet and shifted the muzzle to the back of his neck. She nodded for Viola to follow, waited for her to zip up her overtrousers, and then shoved the driver towards the door. He stumbled over the lip of the door and sprawled onto the snow. Natuk knelt on his back, forcing the air out of his lungs as she pressed the muzzle into the back of his head.

"You can't kill me," he said.

"Why not?"

"If you kill me, people will know. They won't follow you anymore."

"They don't have to follow me," Natuk said. "Just her." She nodded at Viola as she stepped out of the doorway.

"Natuk," Viola said. "What are you going to do?"

"Hey, girl," the driver said. He squirmed beneath Natuk's knee to look at Viola. "I wasn't going to hurt you. You know that. Right?"

"Shut up," Natuk said. She gritted her teeth, as a ripple of energy shuddered through her body.

"*Girl*, believe me."

"That's enough."

Viola stepped over the lip of the door. She reached out to touch Natuk's shoulder, only to recoil as Natuk pushed her away. The driver felt the shift in Natuk's weight and he twisted beneath her, reaching for the pistol. Natuk bounced onto her heels, slipping on the ice as the driver reared up above her.

"No," Viola shouted.

Natuk fell onto her back and fired. The first bullet went through the driver's stomach and he buckled above Natuk's head. She straightened her arms and fired twice, snapping the driver's head backwards. His body flipped in the air. Viola pressed her hands to her mouth at the sound of the man's head slamming into the side of the car. His body slid down the door and crumpled in the snow as Natuk rolled onto her knees and stood up. She slipped the pistol into the waistband of her trousers and grabbed the driver's trousers at his ankle.

"Help me, Viola," she said.

Together they dragged the driver's body around the side of the house and rolled it into the shadow behind the empty oil tank.

"You just gonna leave him there?" the man from the house asked. "The neighbours is going to find him. Then they is going to come looking for me." He spat on the snow. "That's not fair," he said.

"No-one's going to find him," Natuk said. "Come tomorrow night, they'll be too busy. You've got the whole winter to hide him."

"It's still not fair," the man said. "I gave you good information, and you is giving me a body in return."

"I paid you plenty," she said. "Enough to hide him." She pointed at the oil tank. "Stick him in there. You don't use it."

The man spat again, glared at Natuk, and then went back inside the house. Viola stared at the driver's body.

"Don't look at him," Natuk said. "He can't hurt you now."

"You killed him."

"He was going to hurt you."

"No," Viola said. She shook her head. "That's not why you killed him. I saw your face. You were trembling."

"It was adrenaline."

"It was more than that," Viola said. "Someone did something to you. Not him. Someone else. They did the same to you that he wanted to do to me." Viola looked at Natuk. "I'm right. That's why you killed him."

Natuk pressed her finger to her face and wiped a spot of blood from her cheek. She stared at the blood on her finger, and then used her sleeve to wipe her face. Viola watched her. Natuk looked up and down the street. She stared at a window in a small apartment block opposite the house. Viola turned to see the curtain move. She thought she saw a face, and then Natuk took her arm and walked her to the car.

"I've got what I need. We have to go."

"No," Viola said. "Not before you answer me." She pulled free of Natuk's grip and took a step away from the car. "I'm not going with you until you tell me."

"Viola…"

"My name is *Tiina*," she said.

"Fine," Natuk said. She pointed at the oil tank and the shadow beside it. "My father abused me when I was a girl. He raped me. More than once. I told myself that once I was strong enough, I would never let it happen again. Not to me. Not to anyone." She stabbed her finger in the air between her and the driver's body. "*He* was going to hurt you. I stopped him," she said. "Now can we go? We have a long night and a long day ahead of us, and I have to go see somebody."

"Someone else?" Viola frowned. "Who?"

"My mother."

Chapter 17

There were devils outside Petra's apartment. She heard them scuffing the floor in the stairwell, stubbing Petra's doormat with oversized boots to match their oversized bodies. Petra paused at the last step and studied the monsters. She took out her key as she watched them begin their dance. One of the devils was tall, adult-sized. Its shoulders were uneven, as was the triangular body that tapered toward its waist. Petra looked at its face, black and sooty. There were red welts crumbling in thick red paint beneath its eyes, and its hair, thick and black, was tied in a tight bun at the very top of the devil's head; small whalebones protruded from it at crazy angles. The second devil was shorter with a more vigorous dance. Its face was masked, not painted, and its hair was pigtailed and pinned with more bones, white against the black mask. The teeth of the mask were stubby and brown, but it was the clawed fingers that impressed Petra the most, as the devil pawed at the air between them, dancing towards Petra and then giggling and shrieking back to the bigger devil at the door.

"I wonder who it is." Petra said. She creased her forehead with an appropriate frown.

The tall devil cocked its head and struck an ungainly pose, while the shorter devil giggled once again.

"I just don't know," Petra said. She took a step towards her apartment door. "Perhaps if I let you in, and find some candy, maybe I will remember your names?"

The devils pawed and clawed at Petra's shoulders

as she unlocked the door. Compared to the devils on the street, the uneven pair with their bulky upper bodies and grotesque faces were a welcome relief. Petra stood back to let them inside.

The shorter devil kicked off her boots and ran to the sofa, shrieking as she climbed up and over the back to roll onto the thick cushions. The other devil shrugged as if she was not responsible for the child-sized devil. Petra laughed and filled a glass bowl with sweets.

"You have to come closer," she said, and beckoned for the shorter devil to come and sit on her lap. Petra placed the bowl of candy on the kitchen table and sat down on a chair beside it, the shorter devil squirmed onto her lap. "Now, who are you?"

When the devil reached for the candy, Petra tickled its stomach. The devil giggled.

"I didn't think you were supposed to say anything," Petra said.

"I'm not," the devil said, and giggled again.

"You just did."

Petra tickled the devil a second time, and its mask slipped down to its nose.

"You're cheating," the devil said, its voice shrill, the words bouncing as it giggled.

"I know who you are," Petra said. "You're not a devil, you're a little boy."

"*Naamik*," the devil said as it squirmed on Petra's thighs.

"Your name is Johannes."

The devil shook its head.

"It's Karl."

"*Naamik*. I'm not a boy."

"Ah, so, you must be Gertrude."

"I'm not Gertrude."

"No," Petra said, as she pulled the devil into a long, tight hug. She pressed her cheeks against the devil's mask and whispered in her ear. "Your name is Quaa," she said.

"*Aap.*" Quaa lifted her mask and pushed it up onto the top of her head. There was soot around her eyes, Petra smeared it with her fingers as she clasped her hands to Quaa's cheeks and kissed her on the nose. Quaa pointed at the tall devil standing behind her.

"That's right. There's another devil in my kitchen," Petra said. "Do you know who she is?"

Quaa shook her head and pushed two wine gums into her mouth.

"I think I do," Petra said, as the other devil stuck out its tongue, raised its arms and twirled around the kitchen. "Hello Iiluuna."

"Finally," Iiluuna said, as she dropped her arms to her side and slumped on a chair at the table.

"It's a good mask," Petra said.

"It will never come off."

"No, it won't." Petra laughed.

"We're a day early," Iiluuna said. "We're flying to Denmark tomorrow. Quaa desperately wanted to visit you on *mitaartut*, so I said we would come today." Iiluuna sighed. "I should have called. I didn't think you would be so late."

"I'm sorry you had to wait, but I enjoyed the surprise." Petra turned Quaa on her knee. "Why are you going to Denmark?"

Quaa looked at Iiluuna. She pushed the sweets around her mouth and waited for her to answer.

"The doctors at Kong Frederik's Hospital found

an Atrial Septal Defect in Quaa's heart. A tiny hole. She's never shown any symptoms, no shortness of breath, but they were checking the kids in Quaa's class for tuberculosis, and they wanted to see Quaa again. They think she has a tiny hole in her heart. The specialist is off sick, but they don't want to wait, so we fly to Denmark tomorrow."

"Hey," Petra said, as she pulled Quaa to her chest. "I'm sorry."

"It's okay," Quaa said. She shrugged. "I can't feel anything."

"They just want to check." Iiluuna reached across the table and took Petra's hand. "She's alright, Piitalaat. Really."

"I know." Petra pressed her cheek against Quaa's hair, sniffing at the familiar coconut shampoo, and hiding her tears in the tangle of Quaa's hair. She pulled back as the tip of a whalebone pressed into her forehead. "Ow," she said. "You're all spiky."

"I'm a monster," Quaa said. "Monsters are spiky."

Petra nodded. She brushed Quaa's cheek with her hand, and then pushed her gently off her lap.

"I'm going to make some coffee," she said. "For the other monster."

Quaa took a handful of candy and skipped to the sofa. Petra watched her and then filled the coffee maker with water.

"She really is okay," Iiluuna said, as she stood up. She pressed her hand on Petra's shoulder and pulled her close.

"I know," Petra said. She pulled her head back as something smeared her cheek. "You're covering me in soot," she said.

"I'll never get it off."

"You know where the bathroom is."

Petra dumped four scoops of coffee into the filter and then pressed her hands on the lid of the coffee can. She took a breath, wiped another tear from her eye, and then pressed the start button. The coffee maker spluttered as the water warmed.

Quaa is going to be alright, Piitalaat.

"I know, David. It's just…"

You're going to be alright.

Petra nodded, dried her eyes, and joined Quaa on the sofa. They found a Christmas film to stream on the wall screen as Iiluuna wiped the soot from her face.

Iiluuna emerged from the bathroom with a grey face and slimmer shoulders. She filled two mugs of coffee and handed one to Petra as she sat down in the armchair next to the sofa. Quaa slid onto Petra's lap, twirling a wheel of liquorice slowly around her finger as her eyelids blinked slower and slower. Petra tugged the whalebones from Quaa's hair and stroked her head until Quaa started to snore.

"She's excited about flying tomorrow," Iiluuna said. "It's her first time to Denmark. I want her to go before…"

"Before we become independent?"

Iiluuna shrugged. "Things will change."

"A lot of things," Petra said. "Are you nervous?"

"*Naamik,*" Iiluuna said. "Not for me." She looked at Quaa. "Maybe a little for her."

"Pipaluk is strong," Petra said. "She'll make it work."

"You think so? I thought you didn't like her."

Petra teased a knot out of Quaa's hair as she

thought for a moment. "We don't always see eye to eye, that's for sure. But I am impressed. She has strength and a sense of conviction. I think she will make a good President."

"President?" Iiluuna laughed. "I suppose we could be a republic."

"If that's what the people want," Petra said. She looked out of the window at the lights of the city just across the fjord. *But I don't know what they want*, she thought, *not really*.

"We should go," Iiluuna said.

"It's okay. You can stay."

"You've got that look in your eye, Piitalaat. I can see you're busy – thinking."

"I have a meeting with the First Minister in the morning." Petra found another knot in Quaa's hair. "I'd like to enjoy tonight. Please stay," she said. "You can sleep in the guestroom. The bed is made up."

"If you're sure?"

"I am."

The Christmas film finished and Iiluuna lifted Quaa from Petra's lap. She carried her into the guestroom and Petra pulled back the covers. She kissed Quaa goodnight and hugged Iiluuna.

"I met you on the saddest day in my life," she said, as she splayed her fingers on Iiluuna's back. "But I'm so pleased you're in my life. David is too, you know, I can feel it."

"I know," Iiluuna said. She smiled as Petra let go.

Petra tidied her hair, smoothing long strands behind her ears.

"I'll be up for a bit," she said. "Reading."

"You're reading David's books?"

"I'm trying." Petra frowned. "They're not really

my thing, but I think it amuses him, wherever he is, that I am trying. Don't worry if you hear me padding about for a bit. I just need to unwind. It's been a long day."

Petra closed the door quietly behind her, topped up her mug of coffee, and found a cold beer in the fridge; she carried both to the armchair, sat down and picked up the book on the table next to the chair.

"This is for you," she whispered, as she glanced upwards.

She read until midnight, cradling the bottle of beer against her chin between sips. She let her coffee cool in the mug on the table. Petra turned another page, frowned at the start of yet another battle in space, and then paused at the sound of her phone vibrating. She put the book down and pulled her mobile out of her pocket. The screen flickered with cascading windows, message boxes glowing with a series of reports of masked people on the streets of Nuuk. Several of the reports indicated that the people were armed with sticks. Petra read a pinned message from Tavik as he called for calm, reminding all the officers on duty that it was January 6th, and *mitaartut* had begun, albeit much earlier than usual.

They're supposed to wait until the evening, Petra thought.

She read a string of three more messages, before opening a fourth from Gaba asking her to call.

"It's late, Gaba," she said, as he answered. "You should be at home."

"Atii is with the boys. She's resting. She wants to be up early."

"We have a meeting…"

"With the First Minister. I know." Gaba paused.

"I told her I was looking for Anna Riis. She pretended not to hear me, but she's focused on finding Natuk now. I thought you might want to know."

"I have a feeling that if you find one, you'll find the other," Petra said.

"This is why I'm calling. I'm pretty sure I can bring in the Ombudsman without too much trouble."

"But you're worried about Natuk?"

"*Aap*," he said.

Petra fidgeted on the chair, tucking her heels beneath her bottom as she considered what Gaba was really asking.

"You want to know how far I'll go," she said.

"I want to know how far you'll let *me* go. What are my limits?"

"Limits?" Petra almost laughed. "I didn't think you had any."

"I don't, that's why I'm calling."

Gaba waited as Petra thought about how well she knew Natuk. Beyond the fact that she was young, intelligent, and committed, Petra realised she didn't know her very well at all. But those three things were enough. Natuk had the energy, the commitment to do anything, and the mental capacity to see it through. Just like her brother, Ooqi. The irony of Gaba being investigated for his role in Ooqi's death as he secretly hunted a woman that might lead him to Ooqi's sister dried Petra's mouth. She took a last sip of beer and pressed her mobile to her ear.

"Gaba," she said.

"*Aap?*"

"Do what you have to do. Just be safe."

"You know me, Petra."

"Yes, and that's what worries me."

Chapter 18

The bow of the trawler bumped through the ice littering the fjord as the captain returned to the dock. Natuk waved at the tall Greenlander on the deck and wrapped her arm around Viola as she shivered beside her. Natuk frowned at the blue tinge to Viola's lips and wondered if she had a fever. It had taken longer to get her away from the bridge than Natuk had anticipated. The snow on the slopes of the mountains was wet and deep. She looked at Viola's boots and wondered if her feet were cold. The leather on the sides and above Viola's toes was darker than the leather around her ankles.

"It's warm on the boat," Natuk said. "You can rest, change your clothes and dry your boots."

"I'm fine."

"We'll see. Not long now."

Natuk let go of Viola as the trawler slowed and bumped along the wooden dock. There was a damp squeal of metal and the slow pop of a rubber fender. Natuk caught the line that Angut cast from the deck and wrapped it once through a cleat. She held one end as Angut helped Viola onboard, and then climbed over the side, letting the line run through her fingers and the cleat as the captain steered the trawler away from the dock towards the mouth of the fjord.

"You did well," Natuk said, as she slapped Angut on the shoulder.

"And you?" he asked. "I heard there was some trouble."

"The bridge?"

"*Naamik*." He shook his head. "Something about one of the drivers."

"I dealt with it." Natuk looked down as she coiled the line at her feet.

"And Qallu?"

"Natsi's going to get back to me, as soon as Qallu comes up for air."

"We should move the drones."

"Not yet," Natuk said. "I want them airborne first, and then we can relocate the computers and the controllers." She gripped Angut's wrist and turned it to look at his watch. "Another hour, then we fly. The batteries will keep them airborne for twenty-four hours. That's long enough."

Natuk smiled at Viola and took a step towards the door to the cabin. Angut caught her arm and stopped her.

"What is it?"

"Your foster mother is below."

"I know. You did well."

"It's not that. She's spooked. I wanted to warn you."

Natuk caught the smile creasing the corner of her mouth and took a breath of cold air to flatten it. The balance of power was shifting, finally. *But it's too soon for her to realise that*, she thought.

"How?"

"How did she get spooked?" Angut shrugged. "I don't know. But when I picked her up, she had just been in a room with the Police Commissioner."

"Petra," Natuk said. She bit her bottom lip as she stared past Viola towards the wide mouth of the fjord. "Of course."

It was just possible that Petra Jensen might be the one person who could see through Natuk. She remembered the way Petra cut through the concerns of the police officers around her and tried to convince everyone that the Calendar Man's terror campaign had nothing to do with her, it wasn't personal, it was a smokescreen. Natuk thought about how she had worked with Ooqi to ensure that Petra and the task force understood the links to Petra's past, and yet, she had still seen through them. Perhaps the only thing that Petra failed to see through was her own belief that Ooqi and Natuk were victims, that someone else was pulling the strings. She was right, of course, Ooqi was acting under orders and increasing pressure from their foster mother. *But I'm not like my brother*, Natuk thought. Anna might have seen it, glimpsed what Natuk has capable of, glimpsed her commitment. Petra would just have to find out the hard way.

Natuk took Viola's hand and led her inside the cabin of the trawler. She caught and held her as the captain turned into a wave, and then helped her down the ladder to the crew quarters below.

"Have a seat, Viola," she said.

Natuk helped Viola out of her jacket. She smiled as she unzipped her salopettes. She would have lingered and taken her time, teasing Viola as she removed more clothing, but she was still unnerved by the incident with the driver.

"He'll never hurt you again," Natuk said.

"I know."

Natuk unlaced Viola's boots, tugged them off her feet and tossed them to one side. She removed Viola's socks, pulling a face as she twisted them in her hands, squeezing water onto the deck below the table.

"Your feet are ice cold," she said. "Come on. Let's find you a bunk. You'll feel better after some sleep, and then a meal and a hot drink."

Natuk opened a thin wooden door and led Viola inside a dingy cabin. There was a soft light glowing above the pillow on the bottom bunk bed. Natuk pulled back the sheets and pressed Viola onto the bed. She tucked the sheets around Viola's body, covering her to the neck, and kissed her forehead, her nose and lips when she was done. Viola took her hand as Natuk turned to leave.

"You said he would never hurt me," Viola said.

"He can't."

"I know, but would you?"

"Me? Would I what?"

"Would you ever hurt me?"

"No," Natuk said. "Never."

She kneeled by the bed and stroked Viola's hair across her cheek.

"It's just, sometimes, you get this look in your eye," Viola said. "It scares me."

"There's nothing to be scared of," Natuk said, although she knew the look Viola had seen. It was the same look she gave herself in the mirror when a little extra effort and commitment were required to get through a difficult day, or an hour, *or the next few minutes*, she thought as she kissed Viola, plucked her fingers from the young woman's grasp, and turned out the light.

Natuk shut the door on the way out of the cabin, caught her reflection in the polished metal sheet screwed into the wall, and saw the look, that steely-eyed glare that gave her a sense of superhuman strength. It gave her the edge she needed to open the door to the next cabin, the one reserved for her foster mother.

"Hello, Anna," she said, as she stepped into the cabin.

The same lamp glowed above the pillow of the bunk in Anna's cabin, as it had in the cabin next door, but the light was lost in the stark and bright illumination of the overhead light, the lamps on the walls, and the flare of light reflected in the mirror. Anna Riis stood in the room, bathed in light from all angles. It shone through the thin cardigan from the detention centre, and Natuk almost gasped at how frail she had become.

"I'm Anna now, am I?" Anna said. "Am I not your mother?"

"You never were."

Natuk closed the door and leaned against it. She studied the firm set of Anna's jaw, right-angled like the sleeves of her cardigan and the crease in her trousers. She might look frail, but she was still as sharp as a razor.

"Ungrateful child. After all I did for you and your brother."

"My brother is dead," Natuk said. "You killed him."

"It wasn't me that pulled the trigger."

"It might as well have been. You put him there."

"For a purpose, Natuk. He had a job to do, just as you do. He failed. What about you? Are you going to fail too?" Anna tensed. She gritted her teeth. The harsh light caught the lines of muscle beneath her thin and pallid skin.

It was a good act, Natuk decided. She almost clapped. *Not yet*, she thought. *I want to see how far she will go.*

"I won't fail," Natuk said. She pushed away from

the door and opened the cupboard. She slipped her hand between two towels and pulled out a pistol. "I'll look after this," she said. "I don't want you to hurt yourself."

"What are you up to, Natuk?" Anna took a slow step towards her. She reached out to touch Natuk's arm, only to let her hand fall as Natuk pulled away. "What are you doing with that girl?"

"You mean Viola?"

"You called her *Viola*?" Anna laughed. "What have I done?" she said. "I knew you were impressionable, you both were, but I never knew just how much."

"What can I say, *mother*? You taught me well."

"I taught you politics, and administration. I taught you how to manipulate and convince people to think one thing while you did another. I taught you the art of deception." Anna stabbed a wrinkled finger towards the bulkhead separating her cabin from Viola's. "I didn't teach you to get someone else to do your dirty work."

"Dirty work?"

"Or whatever else it is you have planned for that pathetic waif."

"You saw her?"

"I saw her picture in the DataStream. I heard the questions she asked at the First Minister's press conference, and I saw her at the bridge wearing the same mask you have plastered all over the city."

"You saw all that from your cell?"

Anna sneered. "That's what's so perverse about this country. I was supposed to be in detention, yet I have access to the news, current events. I saw your first moves, Natuk. I watched them develop."

"And what about now?"

Anna pressed her lips together. She looked over her shoulder and sat on the edge of the bed. She watched as Natuk removed the magazine from the pistol and the bullet from the chamber. Natuk tossed the magazine and the bullet onto the bed. She slid her right hand to the stop beneath the sights and gripped the tear-down switches with the fingers of her other hand. She pulled the pistol apart and tossed the parts onto the bed.

Natuk stared at her foster mother. "I asked you a question, *mother*."

"Is that supposed to impress me?" Anna said. "That you can handle a gun?"

"It's not the only thing I can handle." Natuk pointed at the bulkhead. "That pathetic girl you mentioned is the face of the new campaign. *My* campaign. She might even be the face of the new Greenland."

"A new Greenland?" Anna scoffed. "What are you talking about? I thought I made it very clear that there is only one thing that can benefit this country, and that is continued influence from Denmark. Your brother understood that. Why can't you?"

"This patriotism of yours," Natuk said. "I don't understand that. I mean, is it rewarded? Do you feel rewarded or maybe even admired or appreciated by your beloved country? I can't see it."

"You can't see the appreciation?" Anna stood up. "Just who do you think funds all this? Your drones, the weapons, this boat. Where do you think the money comes from?"

"It's not the Danish government."

"Of course not, stupid child. Really, Natuk, I

thought you were smarter than that. Now I realise I was stupid to worry. Clearly, Ooqi was the more intelligent twin. It's such a shame that he died, and now it's up to you to complete his work."

Natuk clenched her fists at her sides. She pressed her teeth together as she glared at Anna.

"You can call me anything you want," she said.

"But not stupid?" Anna laughed. "Stupid children think that governments support radical campaigns, when really it is far more complex than that. You won't find any links to the Danish government in any of the supplies you have received. But neither will you hear them denounce Greenland's independence games in public. They have to be seen to be supportive. It's all about public opinion and popularity. But the real agenda can be seen beneath the surface, or even in the cabin of a fishing trawler, if people knew where to look." Anna reached out and brushed her hand against Natuk's face. "Child," she said. "My child. I was rash. Forgive me. Let's start again. Tell me what you have planned, and what progress you have made. I can see you have been busy, and I am sure that the girl is a crucial part of your campaign. She has already put the First Minister on the back foot and should be commended for that. You both should. I know it was you that orchestrated it. I just want to understand why. Tell me so I can reassure our backers."

"You want me to tell you everything?" Natuk asked.

"I want you to convince me that you are on the right path. Because for a moment, I was concerned that you had strayed."

"Did the Commissioner make you think that?"

Anna frowned. "How did you know about that?"

"Angut."

"Yes, of course." Anna nodded. "He is more perceptive than I imagined." She sat down and swept the gun parts to one side. "Sit with me, Natuk. Tell me everything. Show me your vision for our Greenland, one that our friends in Denmark can be proud of."

"I can bring you up to speed," Natuk said, as she sat down. *But it's not your vision for our Greenland anymore*, she thought. *It's mine.*

Marlunngorneq

Tuesday, 6th January 2043
Mitaartut

Chapter 19

Gaba bumped his car over the ridge of ice by the side of the road and parked in a space between the drifts of snow on the street. He turned off the engine and lowered the window. The sound of chanting drifted along the street from the main road, Gaba could just see the blur of masked figures passing the entrance, he noted the sticks and baseball bats they carried. Gaba opened the glove compartment and took out the extendable police baton. He would prefer a pistol, but the inquiry into Ooqi Kleemann's death was ongoing, and Gaba decided the chance of being caught with a pistol was not worth the risk of jeopardizing the outcome. *If this crowd gets ugly*, he thought, *I'll just have to get physical*. Gaba smiled at the thought. He slipped the baton into the inside pocket of his jacket, closed the window and opened the door. The sound of chanting and jeering was louder now, and the crowd passing the street entrance was denser. *Mitaartut* had begun.

"About twelve hours too early," Gaba said, as he closed the car door.

Gaba jogged to the end of the street and then slipped into the crowd. He took the baton out of his jacket and jerked it to its full length. One of the crowd nodded at the baton and then pointed at Gaba's face.

"Where's your mask?"

The mask obscured the person's mouth and muffled their words, but the deep tones suggested it was a man. Gaba paused for a second to study the man's body and noted the thick leather jacket he wore over a fleece hoodie. The man carried a length of metal that looked like a railing from a fishing boat.

"I left it at home," Gaba said.

"Talk to Kuupik, he's got loads in his pack."

"Right." Gaba gestured at the group flowing around them like a steam of armoured fish around an island of coral. "Which one."

"He's the one with the red backpack." The man laughed. "All the leaders have red backpacks. Didn't you read the message in the DataStream?"

"I must have missed it."

The man leaned in close to Gaba, tilting his head as if the mask restricted his vision.

"You're a little old for this."

"But young at heart," Gaba said. "Red backpack?"

"Over there." The man pointed. "At the back of this group.

Gaba estimated that *this group* included about thirty people. All of them were armed and wore some kind of padded top, varying in size and thickness. They wouldn't stop a bullet but might deflect the first or second strike of a police baton, giving enough time for a second wave or *group* of demonstrators to rush the police line. Gaba wondered if the police had enough officers to form a line, and where? Just one group of thirty could close a street. It wouldn't take many groups to shut down the city.

This is going to get ugly, he thought.

The man in the mask drifted away, and Gaba pushed his way through the group to the man wearing a red backpack. He walked at the rear, with the next group about two hundred metres behind him. They rounded the corner in the main road as Gaba approached him.

"Kuupik?" Gaba asked.

"*Aap.*"

"I need a mask."

Kuupik stopped walking, shrugged the backpack off his back and unzipped it. Gaba glanced up and down the road. As Kuupik reached into the backpack, Gaba hooked his arm around the shorter man's neck and dragged him into the shadows between two buildings. Gaba kicked Kuupik's legs and dropped him to the floor. He pulled the mask off Kuupik's face, as he pressed his knee into the young man's chest.

"What's your last name?"

"What?"

"Your last name, *idiot*. What is it?"

"Heilmann."

"That's better," Gaba said. He lifted his knee a little to let Kuupik breathe. "What's in the backpack?"

"Masks."

"Anything else? Any weapons?"

Kuupik shook his head.

"You're sure? What about a knife? If I find anything in there, it's just going to make me mad. This…" Gaba pressed his knee into Kuupik's sternum. "This is just mildly irritated. I guarantee you don't want to see me mad." He lifted his knee and Kuupik gasped cold air into his lungs.

"I've got flares," Kuupik said.

"Like signal flares?" Gaba opened the backpack.

"*Aap.*"

Gaba emptied the backpack onto the snow beside Kuupik's head. The sound of the second group approaching turned Gaba's head. He gripped Kuupik's jacket and dragged him deeper into the shadows, pressing both knees onto the man's chest as the first of the group passed the entrance to the alleyway. When the last member of the group – a short person carrying a red backpack – disappeared out of sight, Gaba released the pressure on Kuupik's chest and let the man breathe. Gaba stabbed the police baton into the snow beside Kuupik's head and leaned close to whisper in the man's ear.

"Don't even think about shouting."

Kuupik shook his head.

Gaba plucked the mask from Kuupik's head, turning it in the light as he studied it. The form was identical to the stack of four masks pressed together in the snow, only the colour was different. Each mask was painted black but with different accents of red smeared beneath bulbous cheeks and twisted lips. It was the same mask pasted onto every public window in Nuuk. Gaba tossed it into the snow.

"How many groups are there, Kuupik?"

"What?"

"Don't make me mad," Gaba said. He slapped Kuupik's cheek.

"Are you police?"

"I'm retired," he said. Gaba smiled at the thought of an old friend who used to say the same.

"Then why do you want to know?"

"That's two questions too many," Gaba said. He slapped Kuupik a second time. "How about you try again. How many groups?"

"Fifteen," Kuupik said.

"And thirty people in each?"

Kuupik nodded.

"About thirty," he said.

Gaba did the math. He plucked the baton from

the snow and tapped Kuupik's head as he counted.

"You're telling me, that there's over four hundred idiots like you with masks and sticks running around in my city?"

Kuupik stared at him, and Gaba tapped his head one more time, hard.

"*Aap*," Kuupik said. "But it's not *your* city. Not for much longer."

"No?"

"We're taking it back."

Kuupik glanced at the baton as Gaba stabbed it into the snow.

"You're taking it back?" Gaba nodded. "Okay, you've got my attention. Enlighten me. Just who are you taking it back from?"

"The corrupt politicians."

"Corrupt?"

"All of them. Especially that bitch, Uutaaq."

"You mean the bitch that has been working towards Greenlandic independence since she left high school? That *bitch*?"

"She's not doing it for us. It's all for her. She just wants the spotlight on her. She wants the rewards too. All the…"

Gaba slapped Kuupik hard. He pressed his fingers into his cheeks, prising his teeth apart.

"See that kind of talk does make me a little mad. But you're entitled to be stupid. I might even forgive you if you co-operate." Gaba relaxed his grip. "You said you are one of the leaders. How about you tell me where I can find your boss?"

Kuupik's face twisted beneath Gaba's grip, his eyes widened. Gaba let go and studied his face. He peered into Kuupik's eyes and leaned in close. Gaba sniffed twice and pulled back.

"You're scared, Kuupik. Is it your boss who scares you? More than I do? Now, that's interesting. How about you tell me about her?"

"I don't know anything," Kuupik said, as Gaba reached for the baton. "Hey, you can hit me as hard as you want, and I still won't know anything."

"You're that scared of him?" Gaba paused as Kuupik looked away. "Or maybe it's not a *he*? Who's your boss, Kuupik? Who's calling the shots?"

"I don't know her name."

"No?" Gaba shifted his knee onto Kuupik's chest.

"I don't." Kuupik gasped for air and Gaba lifted his knee. "I don't even know where she is. Not in Nuuk. Not all the time. We get messages in the DataStream. If we meet with anyone, it's her partner."

"Her partner?" Gaba reached for the baton.

"He's our contact. His name is Angut," Kuupik said, his voice louder.

Gaba glanced over his shoulder, and then leaned closer.

"Angut *who*?" he asked.

"Just Angut."

"Describe him."

"Tall, like you," Kuupik said. "And mean…"

"Like me?" Gaba laughed. "I'm actually beginning to like you, Kuupik. Maybe I'll let you go, so you can have some fun with your friends tonight. If you just tell me a little more, a few details. We'll keep it between you and me." Gaba lowered his voice. "Angut doesn't need to know. Neither does your boss. What was her name? Natuk, maybe?"

Gaba smiled as Kuupik squirmed beneath him.

"How do you know her name?" he asked.

"So, I'm right?"

"I didn't say that," Kuupik said. "I didn't say anything."

"No," Gaba said. "I have to do all the work."

Gaba cursed at a sudden crick in his knee and shifted his weight to one side. Kuupik felt him move and grabbed a handful of snow. He cast it into Gaba's face as he jerked his body to one side and rolled free of Gaba's body. Kuupik scrambled to his feet. He turned and kicked Gaba in the chest as the older man rocked back onto his heels. Kuupik sprinted for the main road as Gaba fell back into the snow.

"That was all kinds of stupid," Gaba said, as he watched Kuupik run around the corner. Gaba picked up the baton and brushed the snow from the shaft. He tucked it into his jacket, slipped a mask over his head, and ran after Kuupik.

Gaba slid at the corner. He grabbed a wooden fence for support and scanned the road. He saw Kuupik flailing with the gait of a weekend warrior. Gaba grinned behind the mask and ran after him. Kuupik looked over his shoulder as Gaba closed the distance between them, stumbling and slipping on the compacted snow, he sprawled onto the road. Gaba grabbed the back of Kuupik's jacket and pulled him to his feet. He pushed him across the road, slapping his head with his free hand.

"I'm mad now, Kuupik," he said.

Slap.

"You know what that means?"

Slap.

Gaba dragged Kuupik around an SUV parked in the snow. He slammed the younger man's body against the side of the car and pressed the palm of his hand beneath his chin, pushing upwards as he spread Kuupik's legs with a swift kick to each ankle.

"You know what people call me?" Gaba said, as Kuupik trembled. "They call me the *pit bull*." Gaba's breath was hot behind the mask and he pushed it up over his face and onto his bald head. "I don't mind the name; it kind of fits," he said. "Something you're about to find out."

"I don't know anything," Kuupik said.

"You're lying."

Gaba pushed Kuupik's head backwards into the snow on the roof of the SUV.

"You've told me how many. Now I want to know where, when… Tell me the plan, Kuupik, or your part in it ends right now, right here."

"They'll kill me if I tell you."

"And I'll kill you if you don't. Your choice."

Gaba turned his head at the sight of a third group of demonstrators. Kuupik followed his gaze and began to laugh.

"You think this is funny?" Gaba said. He pressed his face close to Kuupik's. "We just have to work faster, that's all." Gaba looked at the group again, judging the distance. There was about forty metres of road between them. Not enough. He let go of Kuupik when the demonstrators at the front of the group began to shout and point.

"Who's the idiot now," Kuupik said, as he slid down the side of the car.

Gaba reached inside his jacket and silenced him with a swift blow from the baton. He extended the baton and then pulled his mobile from his pocket. Gaba swiped through the list of contacts and pressed

Petra's avatar. He pressed his mobile to his ear and started to run.

"Petra," he said, when she answered. "We've got a problem."

Chapter 20

The broad utility belt pressed down on Natuk's hips as she slipped the regulation Heckler and Koch USP Compact pistol into the holster and her own FNS 40 into a holster strapped above her left ankle. Natuk adjusted the belt, tugged her police sweater over the light blue shirt and pulled her jacket off the hook beside the bathroom mirror. She stared at her reflection as she pulled on the jacket. She had worn the uniform for much of her adult life, and, regardless of her foster mother's ulterior motives, Natuk had been proud to wear it, and privately pleased with the role of keeper of the peace in Greenland. *Except now, on my birthday*, she thought, *I intend to disturb that peace in the worst way.* Natuk zipped her jacket and stepped out of the bathroom, it was time to wake Viola.

Natuk stepped lightly into Viola's cabin. She held her breath as she watched her sleep, pushing a darker stream of thoughts from her mind. Natuk stooped beneath the cot, and pressed her lips to Viola's forehead. She kissed her nose and brushed her cheek, sitting down on the bed as Viola stirred. Natuk smoothed Viola's hair against her head and smiled as Viola opened her eyes.

"What time is it?"

"Early."

Viola blinked as she propped herself up on one elbow. The smile on her lips faded as she looked at Natuk. "Why are you looking at me like that?"

"Like what?"

"Like you're sad or something."

"I'm not sad," Natuk said.

"But you look it."

Natuk leaned over and kissed Viola on the lips, teasing Viola's bottom lip between her teeth. She pulled away and stood up.

"I promised you breakfast," she said. "You've got five minutes."

"Ah, you're so evil," Viola said.

Natuk paused at the door. "Am I?" she whispered.

She turned away as Viola slipped her slim legs over the side of the bed and walked into the kitchen area. The door to her foster mother's cabin was closed, locked from the outside. Natuk allowed herself a smile at the thought. She had busted her out of the detention centre only to lock her away onboard the trawler. She remembered arguing the logic with Angut, that it was a matter of control.

"Timing is key if the play is to be a success," she had said. "I need all the actors to perform their lines at the precise moment. I can't do that if they are beyond my reach."

Angut had grunted something about him just being an actor in some stupid play, but Natuk had ignored him, just as he was ignoring her now, choosing to stay up top with the Captain, leaving Natuk and the women below decks.

"It's just as well," she said, as she turned the eggs on the pan. She pressed two slices of bread into the toaster. "There's no use complicating things by giving him more lines."

"What about *lines*?" Viola asked. She squirmed onto the bench seat and slid into the corner. Viola rested one arm on the table as she picked at a crumb of sleep in the corner of her eye. Natuk pulled a pair of thick-rimmed glasses from her jacket pocket and slid them across the table.

"I've prepared your speech," she said, as she carried two plates of bacon, eggs and toast to the table. "Just put your glasses on. You'll find the icon at the bottom of the lens on the right.

"These things give me a headache," Viola said.

"You get used to it."

Natuk made coffee as Viola ate. She listened as the younger woman rehearsed a little of the speech, encouraging her with tips for more stress on some of the words, less on others.

"Is this what you believe?" Viola asked when she was finished. She let the autocorrect function adjust the lenses to compensate for her eyesight and looked at Natuk.

"*Aap.*"

"You think the current government is corrupt."

"Corrupt or corrupted," Natuk said. "It's the same thing."

"But why do you want me to say it? Why not you?"

Natuk smiled. She handed Viola a mug of coffee and then gestured at her police jacket. "Look at me, Viola. I represent the *system*. I can't make that speech."

"Then take it off."

"Now?" Natuk raised her eyebrows. "Here?"

"You know what I mean," Viola said. She turned the mug on the table, as if searching for words with each revolution. "I just don't understand why it has to be me?"

"Because you're the face of the future." Natuk slid onto the seat beside Viola. She took her hand. "You're young, pretty and strong."

"I'm a student."

"You're clever, smart…"

"I'm going to be a journalist."

"The voice of the people."

A strand of Viola's hair slipped across her cheek as she shook her head. "I've got nothing to say."

"They'll listen anyway," Natuk said. She brushed the hair from Viola's cheek. "Stick to the speech. You can read it from the glasses. I'll be with you, in the DataStream, in the left lens."

"You're not going to be with me? I mean, physically?" Viola pushed away from Natuk and pressed her finger into Natuk's chest, the jacket pillowed at her touch. "Why are you wearing a uniform?"

"We each have our parts to play today. This is mine."

"A police officer?"

"Representing the system and the government, yes."

"I don't understand." Viola took off the glasses and pointed at the DataStream on the lens. "You created all this. You've got people protesting all over the city. It should be you leading the people. You're the one they will follow. Not me."

"You're wrong, Viola. But you're also right, about some things at least. I might be able to pull some strings, but I can't do everything. Once people find out that I am a police officer, then all this will be for nothing. I can't let that happen. I need you to lead them…"

"I can't…"

"Yes, you can. Just far enough for them to begin to lead themselves. This is about giving power to the people, giving them the chance to ask questions and make demands. It's all about the future, Viola, a future you can give them. They'll listen to you. They'll follow you, and, when they're ready, they will take matters into their own hands."

"When will that be?"

"Soon," Natuk said. "Sooner than you think."

"They'll take over?"

"*Aap*. I promise you they will."

"How?"

Natuk bit her bottom lip. She stared at Viola and said, "Don't think about it. Not now." Natuk slid off the seat and stood up. She glanced at the door to Anna's cabin, and then pointed at Viola's jacket hanging from a hook on the bulkhead between the cabins. "It's cold outside," she said.

Viola pushed her mug to one side and slid around the seat. She crossed the deck and stuffed her arms into her thick quilted jacket.

"What about my mask?" she said, pointing at the mask on the hook.

"You won't need it today," Natuk said, stuffing the mask into the cargo pocket of her trousers.

Natuk pulled on her boots and tied the laces as she waited for Viola to do the same. When Viola nodded that she was ready, Natuk took her hand and led her up the stairs to the wheelhouse. She whispered to Angut that they were ready and told the Captain to stay at the dock until she got back. Angut stopped her at the door.

"You haven't seen the feed?" he asked, tapping the rim of his glasses.

"What about?"

"Natsi's been trying to contact you. He found

him."

"Qallu?" Natuk said.

"*Aap*. He's got a room at the Hotel Hans Egede. The night porter saw him."

Natuk dipped her head once at Angut, and then opened the door to the deck. Viola cringed at the sudden breath of cold that flicked at the loose strands of hair beneath her hat. Natuk took a deep breath and stepped over the lip of the door. She beckoned for Viola to come, and then led her down the gangplank to the SUV parked beside the dock.

"We have a short stop to make," she said, as she climbed in behind the wheel and Viola sat down on the passenger seat. "Stay in the car and rehearse your speech."

Natuk drove to the hotel, turning quickly onto a back road to avoid a group of masked revellers marching down the street and parked around the back. Viola shivered as Natuk opened the car door.

"You'll be fine," Natuk said. "Just rehearse your lines."

"Where will you be?"

"There's something I have to do. It won't take long."

Natuk closed the door and jogged around the car to the hotel's rear entrance. She waved her police ID card at the camera and waited for the night manager to buzz her in.

"Can I help you, officer?" he said, as Natuk approached the desk.

"I need to leave a message for one of my colleagues."

The night manager nodded and tapped the screen of his computer to open a new document. "What's the message?" he asked.

"It's more of a *thing*," Natuk said. She pulled Viola's mask from her pocket and placed it on the night manager's desk. "It's evidence. They'll know what to do with it." Natuk shrugged as the night manager frowned at the mask. "I'm on a call. I don't have the time to get it to the station. The duty officer said I could leave it here on my way."

"You can't take it up to your colleague?"

"I don't have time. They know it's here. I'm sure they'll be down soon to pick it up."

The night manager turned his head and looked out of the window. Natuk nodded as he gestured at the revellers passing on the street.

"*Aap*," she said. "It's related." Natuk tapped the desk and took a step backwards.

"I'll send the night porter up and ask your colleague to come down and pick it up."

"It's important that they collect it. I trust you to give it them personally."

"You can rely on me."

"*Qujanaq*," Natuk said. She walked towards the rear entrance, and, when the night manager turned away, she slipped into the hall and pressed the button for the elevator. Natuk stepped inside as the doors opened and slipped her glasses onto her face. She found the message from the porter in the DataStream. Qallu had a room on the fourth floor. Natuk pressed the button for the third. She turned her head away from the camera in the ceiling of the elevator, flicked her eyes onto the messaging icon and dialled Assa at the store.

"What do you need?" he asked.

"I'm at Hotel Hans Egede. I need you to loop the

security feed from all cameras thirty minutes ago. A ten-minute loop should be sufficient."

"You want me to patch it in now?"

"*Aap*. Override the recording function and erase the last ten minutes and the next five."

"Is that all you need?"

"That's all."

Natuk slipped her glasses into her pocket as the elevator slowed. She peered into the corridor as the elevator doors opened. Natuk stepped into the corridor and checked the display above the elevator as the doors closed. She waited for it to continue to the fourth floor and then took the stairs. Natuk saw the police officer guarding Qallu's door step into the elevator on the fourth floor. She waited for the doors to close and then drew the FNS 40 pistol from her ankle holster. Natuk stood to one side of the door to Qallu's room and knocked. She took a breath as he padded to the door. She breathed out as he opened it.

"What is it?" he said, as he looked out of the room.

Natuk twisted around the door and slapped Qallu's chest with the palm of her hand. She pointed the pistol at his head as he recoiled into the room. She slapped him again, harder, forcing him onto his bed. Natuk grabbed a pillow from the chair beside the desk and pressed it against Qallu's chest as she straddled his body. Natuk shoved the barrel of the pistol into the pillow and fired once before moving the pillow and firing a second time into Qallu's face. Natuk took a second to search for the bullet casings, slipping them into her jacket pocket as she stepped off Qallu's body and walked to the door. She stepped into the corridor and closed the door softly behind her. Natuk slipped the pistol into the ankle holster, walked down the corridor and took the stairs to the rear entrance of the hotel. She opened the door and jogged to the car.

"That was quick," Viola said, as Natuk closed got in and closed the driver's door.

"Yep."

"Are you alright?"

"I'm fine."

Natuk glanced in the mirror, saw a spot of blood on her cheek and wiped it off with the back of her hand. She started the engine and pulled away from the hotel.

"Where are we going now?" Viola asked.

"To join the demonstration. It's time for you to make your speech."

Chapter 21

Petra wrote a note for Quaa and her mother as she drank her morning coffee. She left it on the kitchen table, grabbed her keys and pulled on her jacket. Petra stopped as she felt the jacket's familiar greasy texture beneath her fingers. *Not today*, she thought, pushing the stray feelings of guilt to one side as she hung Maratse's old police jacket on the hook and took her own. She left the apartment and locked the door before she could change her mind.

The bus was busier than she had expected, but then most people were back at work now, and school would start soon. Petra stared through the stencil of the mask on the window at the dirty snow lining the street. Someone had tried to remove the stencil, but the image remained, only thinner, more translucent. Petra pressed the button to get off the bus as it neared Hotel Hans Egede. She stepped out of the middle door and into a shallow drift of snow, zipped her jacket to her chin and walked towards the entrance. A shout and the clump of a car door shutting turned her head.

"Don't you have a car?" Seabloom asked as he negotiated a patch of ice between his car and Petra.

"I like the bus," she said. "It makes me feel closer to the…"

"City?"

"I was going to say people, but I guess it's the same." Petra waited for Seabloom to join her. "Is this a pleasant coincidence or are you here on business?"

"Business? I don't know about that, but it is always a pleasure to see you, Petra."

Petra shook her head slightly, shaking thick

snowflakes from her hair and a small flurry of guilty thoughts from her mind. *It's too soon*, she thought.

I was sick for a long time, Piitalaat.

"I know, but…"

"What do you know?" Seabloom asked.

"Nothing," Petra said. She started to say more but stopped at the sight of a group of people in masks at the top of the street. *Aqqusinersuaq* rose slightly in elevation from the hotel to the Post Office at the top of a small hill, and a group of about thirty people stood to one side of the street. It looked like they were waiting for something and Petra wondered if the officers on the night shift knew about them. She spotted a patrol car on the opposite side of the street. Petra checked her watch. It was close to the end of their shift.

"You've seen them then?" Seabloom said.

"Just now."

"They are all over the city. They're wearing the same masks as the protestors on the bridge." He gestured at his car with a wave of a thickly-mittened hand. "We've ratcheted the base security up a notch, and I have three men in the car, including the driver." Seabloom turned to look at the masked figures on the hill. "What do you think?"

"It's a little early for *mitaartut*," Petra said. She smiled at the thought of Quaa and Iiluuna surprising her the evening before. They were early too, but the figures on the hill didn't move, making them that bit more sinister.

"What?"

"It's a tradition. Normally, I wouldn't be worried, but they're not supposed to be out before the evening, and they usually don't go around in such big groups."

"Well, they've spooked your neighbours. We passed guards on the road in and out of Chinatown and Little Amsterdam. I think the incident at the bridge has everyone on edge." Seabloom grinned. "Which is a good thing."

"It is?"

"Based on the unrest we experienced yesterday, I was able to tap into a whole new budget. The three guys in the car are just one part of it."

"I don't understand," Petra said.

"It means the US Coast Guard is ready to assist. I'm here to help, Petra," he said. "I think your First Minister will be pleased to hear that." He nodded at the hotel. "Shall we go inside?"

"You're here to meet with Pipaluk?"

"I've been summoned," Seabloom said. He waited for Petra to walk inside the building and walked beside her to the lift. The night manager waved at her from behind his desk.

"Excuse me," he said. "May I speak with you for a moment?"

"I'll be right there," Petra said to Seabloom. She walked to the desk as he waited by the lift.

"Is this about the First Minister?" Petra asked. "I'm supposed to meet her in her suite."

"No, Commissioner," the night manager said. Colour rushed to his cheeks. "I wasn't thinking. I thought you were a police officer."

"I *am* a police officer," Petra said. She glanced at the man's hands as he tucked something into one of the alcoves on the desk. "What's that?"

"It's a mask. I thought you had been sent to pick this up. The officer said the station would send someone to collect it. He wasn't supposed to leave the hotel."

"Slow down," Petra said, and held up her hand. "Which officer?"

"The one guarding the room on the fourth floor."

"The First Minister is on the fifth floor." Petra frowned. She turned as Seabloom approached the desk, switching to English to explain the situation.

"So, your officer is guarding the wrong door?"

"No," the duty manager said. His English was broad and soft like Seabloom's. "There are currently two officers guarding rooms in the hotel. The First Minister is in one of them. I apologize for any confusion."

"And the second?" Petra asked.

"I don't know his name."

"His?"

"Yes. The police officer on the fourth floor is guarding a man."

"And he told you that someone would be in to pick up the mask?"

"The police officer did, yes." The night manager sighed. "My shift is nearly over. I'm sorry, it has been a long night. What with the breach in our security and…"

"What breach?" Seabloom asked.

"We have lost ten minutes of video footage," the night manager said. "He tapped the mask. "Actually, it was about the time that the police officer delivered this."

"Another police officer?"

"Yes, a woman."

"Can I see it?" Petra held out her hand and the

night manager gave her the mask. She turned it in her fingers and tugged a single short hair from beneath the elastic strap. "Blonde," she said, as she held it up to the light. "I'll take this with me." Petra studied the mask as she walked to the elevator.

"You need a bag for that hair?" Seabloom asked. "An evidence bag," he said, as Petra frowned.

Petra shook her head and tucked the hair inside a small zipped pocket on the front of her jacket. She turned the mask towards Seabloom as he pressed the button for the fifth floor.

"It's the same as the stencil," she said.

"It's pretty ugly."

Petra smiled as she held it up in front of her face. The elevator stopped, and the doors opened, followed by a shriek. Petra lowered the mask to see the First Minister take a step back into the corridor.

"Commissioner," she said, as she recovered. The police officer beside her hid a smile behind his hand. "You're late. I was just on my way down to see if you were in the lobby."

"I thought we should meet in your suite?"

Petra lowered the mask and shot a look at the officer. He took a second to compose himself and then stepped back into the corridor.

"Well, now you're here," Pipaluk said, "we may as well continue." She stepped into the elevator, nodding at Seabloom as he made space for her. The police officer squeezed in as Petra moved back.

"We're not meeting in your suite?" she asked.

"I want to introduce you to someone first," Pipaluk said.

"On the fourth floor?"

"How did you know?"

"First Minister," Petra said. "How you manage your own people is up to you but assigning police officers to special duties is way beyond your remit." Petra unzipped her jacket as the elevator warmed up with the heat of four bodies. The elevator doors opened, and she followed the police officer into the corridor.

"I made an executive decision," Pipaluk said, as she exited the elevator. "I have that privilege."

"Not with my people, you don't." Petra spotted the police officer guarding a room at the end of the corridor. She walked towards him.

"Exceptional circumstances demand immediate action," Pipaluk said. "I found myself in an exceptional situation and I acted. Which is far more than I can say about you and your police force, *Commissioner*. If the rumours of your pending retirement are true, I suggest you hurry it along before I'm forced to make more decisions without your knowledge."

"You can't…"

"Can't I?" Pipaluk stopped outside the door, shoving the police officers to one side with a single look. "Once this country is truly independent, I think you'll find there are many things I can do, with or without your knowledge."

"Excuse me," Seabloom said. "I might not have understood a word of what you have been *discussing*." Seabloom let the last word linger before adding, "But I would like to know why I am here, and what we're doing outside this hotel room?"

Pipaluk changed her tone and softened the smile on her face. She took a moment and then lifted her hand to the door to knock. She knocked three times.

"My assistant was given a tip yesterday. The man in this room came to us with information about the ringleader of this little uprising." Pipaluk gestured at the mask in Petra's hand. "He was concerned for his own safety, and I took the decision to protect him."

"How long have you had this information?" Petra asked.

"I haven't got it yet. He wanted to be assured of his safety before telling me."

"Telling you what?" Seabloom asked.

"The name of the ringleader." Pipaluk's forehead creased as she knocked on the door a second time. "I can't believe he is sleeping. We promised to put him on a plane to Denmark a few hours from now." She stepped back as the police officer entered a code into the number pad on the door. He drew the pistol from his holster a second after he opened the door.

"First Minister," Petra said. "I think you should wait with your protection officer."

Seabloom unsnapped the buttons of his coat and pulled a large pistol from a shoulder holster. He followed the police officer inside the room.

"Ma'am, I think you'd better see this."

Petra stepped into the room, squinting in the darkness. She reached for the switch on the wall and turned on the light. There was relatively little blood compared to the mess one might expect from the bullet holes in the man's head and chest. Petra looked at the pillow tossed to one side when Seabloom pointed at it.

"A silencer?" he said, with a shrug.

"Call it in," Petra said to the officer. "First Minister, would you come in here, please."

"Petra," Seabloom said. "Is that smart?"

"She took an executive decision. I think she should see the consequences."

Pipaluk pressed her hand to her mouth as she stepped into the room. She looked at Petra and turned to leave.

"Not yet," Petra said, as she took the First Minister's hand. "I want you to look at him."

"But your police officer was outside the door," Pipaluk said, her voice quieter than it had been in the corridor. "He's your responsibility."

"And *he* was yours," Petra said with a wave at the dead man on the bed. "If I had known about this, I could have protected him down at the station."

"He didn't want the police to be involved."

"Well, they are now," Seabloom said. He opened his coat and slid the large pistol back into the holster. He flicked his gaze to the media screen mounted on the wall as it turned itself on and the image of the protestors at the top of the street flickered into focus. "What's that?"

A young woman's voice drifted into the room, and the rooms above, opposite and to each side of them as all the media screens in every room of the hotel tuned into the same broadcast.

"That's the girl from the press conference," Pipaluk said.

Petra watched as the young woman, the only one not wearing a mask, stood in front of a group of what looked like hundreds of protestors.

"My name is Viola," she said, as she brushed a snowflake from the lens of her thick-rimmed glasses, "and I have something to say."

Chapter 22

A fresh wind curled a cloud of snow from the rooftop above the back of the nightclub, dumping it on top of Gaba Alatak as he pressed his body against the wall. A group of revellers ran past, the soles of their winter boots thudding across the hard snow pressed into the road, their breath streaming through the holes in their masks like dragon steam. Gaba waited until they had passed, brushed the snow from his shoulders and head, and then stepped out from beneath the roof and onto the street. The corners of his lips wrinkled as he remembered running down a similar street in his youth as the older boys in the town chased him on *mitaartut*. Gaba struggled to remember if it was thirty-five or forty years ago. Probably both. He let the memory linger as far as the corner of the street.

The sounds of the revellers disappeared as he moved deeper into a residential area, further from the centre of Nuuk, and further from the more affluent areas. The grey dawn pushed the black of night into the shadows and cast an eerie light onto the tired apartment blocks, smaller wooden houses, and one L-shaped house in particular. Gaba wiped a soft clump of snow from his bushy eyebrows and stared at what looked like a man dragging a body by the ankles. Gaba almost laughed as he realised the man was wearing some kind of Japanese housecoat. His long hair was bound in a bun at the back of his head, and smoke poured from his lips as he huffed his way across the snow surrounding the house, ploughing a line to the road with the torso and head of the body.

Drunk, Gaba thought, and then he saw the trail of blood in the snow. He took several quiet steps towards the man and then stopped beside a car, waiting for the man to drag the body towards him.

"Natsi?" Gaba said, as the man drew close enough for him to recognise him. "Natsi Hermansen?"

Natsi let go of the dead man's ankles. The cigarette fell from his lips and smoked on the snow as he squinted at Gaba and then looked left and right as if he might start to run.

"Don't," Gaba said.

Natsi darted to the right. Gaba leaped forwards and planted the sole of his boot on the tail of Natsi's housecoat, stopping the middle-aged man in his tracks as he slipped and fell onto the ground. Gaba loomed over him and knelt beside him.

"I told you not to run."

"But you're a cop." Natsi's eyes darted to the left where the body lay in the snow.

"I used to be," Gaba said. He pointed at the body. "Who's your friend?"

"Not my friend. Never met him before tonight."

"No?" Gaba shook his head. "So, you killed a man the very first time you met him? That's not very nice, *Nasty*."

"No-one calls me that anymore."

"But no-one knows you like I do."

Natsi started to rise but Gaba placed his hand on his chest.

"I have a few questions."

"I'm cold."

"Then answer them quickly."

Natsi sighed and lay back in the snow.

"Who killed him?"

"A woman."

"When?"

"Earlier."

"Why?"

"I don't know. I just walked into the living room and she had a gun to his head, shouting. I think he tried to get it on with her friend." Natsi shivered for a second before he continued. "She was with this girl."

"Girl?"

"Young. Twenty-years-old, maybe."

"Okay, now I'm confused, Natsi. Start again. Were there two women?"

"*Aap.*"

"One of them was about twenty?"

"And she was the one he tried to screw," Natsi said. He jerked his thumb towards the dead body.

"And the other woman? You know her?"

Natsi nodded his head.

"What's her name?"

"Natuk."

Gaba looked away as he mouthed the name. Natsi tried to sit up, but he pushed him down again.

"Describe her."

"About twenty-five. Pretty, or she used to be, before she did her hair blonde."

"And how do you know her?"

"We had business together. She used to come around before. She'd help me out if I needed it, I returned the favour."

"What kind of help did you need?"

"You know, man, like when I had trouble with you and your kind."

"Police?"

"*Aap.*" Natsi laughed. "It was crazy, man. I mean she was one of you."

Gaba stood up and pulled Natsi to his feet. He nodded at the body, and said, "Where are you taking it?"

"I was going to put it in the skip, so no-one pinned it on me."

Gaba dipped his head and stared at Natsi. He pointed at the track of red snow leading from the house to the road.

"Shit, man, I'm not stupid. It's snowing. Now's the time to move it." He kicked one of the ankles. "You could help."

"Natsi."

"Sure, man," Natsi said. "If you help, then I'll tell you where to find Natuk. I can see you want to know. You've got that look in your eye, the old Sergeant Gaba hunting look. Everyone knows it. And I can see you got it bad for this girl. She's crazy like you. You'd make a good pair. Maybe you want to get it on and…"

Gaba clasped his hand around Natsi's thin throat. He choked the last of Natsi's sentence with a firm squeeze.

"I think you're going to tell me what you know, and then you're going to call the police." He loosened his grip. "Understand?"

"*Aap.*"

Gaba waited. Natsi looked down at the dead man's feet, then at Gaba, and down again.

"You're kidding?"

Natsi shook his head and Gaba let him go. He grabbed one of the dead man's ankles and waited for Natsi to do the same. Natsi smiled as they dragged the body towards the rubbish skip.

"Stop smiling, Natsi."

"I can't help it," he said, and laughed. "It just feels so good to be working together for a change, Sergeant."

Gaba let go of the body and pulled his mobile out of his pocket. He dialled Petra's number as Natsi rolled the dead body up against the skip.

"Petra?" Gaba said, as she answered. "I've got a lead on Natuk. She's..." Gaba reached out to slap Natsi's arm. "Where's Natuk?"

"She's on a boat," Natsi said. "If she's not in the city."

"In Nuuk?"

"*Aap*. A fishing trawler. She moves around, but I seen her once down by the old dock."

Gaba took a step away from Natsi and pressed the phone against his ear. "She might be on a trawler at the other end of town. Can you send a patrol?"

"Did you say *might*," Petra said.

"What's that noise?" Gaba's forehead creased as he concentrated. "It sounds like you're in a crowd."

"Of protestors, yes. The city is full of them. We're stretched thin again, Gaba. I need everyone I've got on duty. I've pulled Atii off the search for the Ombudsman and Natuk."

"Listen, Petra, I'll check it out. I'll call if I find anything."

The call ended and Gaba stared at his phone. He looked up, tilting his head towards the centre of the city as the sound of shouting and chanting drifted towards him.

"The city's falling apart," Natsi said, and grinned.

Gaba glanced at the dead body and stabbed his finger into Natsi's chest.

"Call it in, today."

"Sure. Later today." Natsi pulled a crumpled packet of cigarettes from his pocket and shook a cigarette out of it. He lit it as Gaba walked away. "Let's do this again, Sergeant," Natsi called out. He grinned again and puffed a cloud of smoke into the snowflakes tumbling onto the street and covering the body by the skip.

Gaba started to jog towards the street on which he parked his car. The sound of hundreds of protestors grew louder as he jogged across a connecting street. He spotted his car, pulled out his keys and slowed to a stop beside it. Gaba opened the door and climbed behind the wheel. His mobile rang as he started the car and he put the call through the speakers.

"This is Gaba," he said, as he drove along the street, turning once, away from the protestors, on his way to the docks in the oldest part of the city, close to the church and the statue of Hans Egede.

"This is officer Aron Ulloriaq. We met in December. I'm the Commissioner's assistant."

"I remember. What do you want, Aron?"

"The Commissioner said you were looking for Natuk. I've been working through the DataStream, trying to find her."

"And?"

"If you're looking for a trawler at the docks, you want one with a hexagon at the top of the mast. It's a Stream booster."

"Like a box?"

"More like a star, open, you can put your hands through it."

"So, like more shrouds?"

"Shrouds?"

"Lines and cables. It won't stand out much, but thanks, anyway." Gaba pressed his finger on top of the button to end the call, and then hesitated. "Aron?"

"*Aap.*"

"Go and find Petra. She needs you."

Gaba ended the call as he spotted the church. He parked the car in the parking area and locked it. He paused to look at the fjord to the right of the church, and then turned his head slowly to the left. Several old wooden buildings obscured his view, but as he started to walk towards the water, he spotted the top of a mast peeping above the roofs. Gaba smiled when he saw thick cables shaped like a hexagon at the top.

"Well done, Aron," he whispered.

He stopped beside a rack of skin-on-frame *qajaq*s in front of the old medical station built in colonial times. Gaba had always been too big to fit inside the tiny round cockpit of a *qajaq*. At least, that's what he would tell people when they asked. The truth had more to do with not wanting to be so close to the water, preferring the stability of a boat to a thin, pointy hunting kayak.

Gaba brushed the snow from the bench next to the rack and studied the trawler. The wheelhouse was lit with a soft red glow and he could see the silhouette of a man sitting in the Captain's chair. The other man, taller with the same build as Gaba, was more interesting. Gaba watched the man walk across the deck to the bow. The distance was too great for details, but the man walked with the attitude of one employed to be the muscle.

"Or leader of the SRU," Gaba said with a smile. "Now, what are you doing onboard that ship and why aren't you in the city stirring up trouble with Natuk and her friends?"

It occurred to Gaba that Natuk might even be below decks on the trawler. *But then she would be missing out on the fun in the city.* He dismissed the thought, and stood up, intending to move closer once the Greenlandic gorilla on the deck returned to the wheelhouse.

Gaba retreated to the shadow of the *qajaq* rack as the grey sky lightened and the snowfall slowed to a light dusting of soft powdery crystals. A second silhouette inside the wheelhouse caught Gaba's eye and he watched as a third person stepped onto the deck. The man at the bow pointed at the wheelhouse. If he had been closer, Gaba imagined he might have heard the man shout something. The third person, a woman, strode defiantly across the deck until the man grabbed her by the shoulders and turned her around.

"Got you," Gaba said, as he caught a glimpse of the woman's face before the man pushed her inside the wheelhouse. It was a brief, but enough to convince Gaba that he had found Natuk's trawler, and he had found Ombudsman Anna Riis. Now all he had to do was get onboard. Gaba straightened at the thought, flexing his fingers in anticipation of another bout of action to stave off the boredom. His childhood memories of *mitaartut* resurfaced, but he tossed them aside in favour of the thought of a bigger, more powerful opponent.

Chapter 23

The city of Nuuk had grown over the years since Petra lived there, first as a child at the children's home, later as a police student, and now as Police Commissioner, but she could not remember ever seeing so many young people gathered in one place at the same time. She did a quick head count of the first row of protestors, ignoring the masks and sticks as she stepped out of the police SUV at the top of *Aqqusinersuaq*. Petra counted just under sixty people in the first row, and, if she stepped onto the bottom rim of the car, she could see four more rows of people behind the first, and a large gathering of people behind the last. They filled the road from the Post Office to the graveyard, blocking traffic, intimidating shoppers, office workers and the few tourists hardy enough to withstand a Greenlandic winter. Only the children seemed unafraid, the school-aged ones, they stared and pointed with wide-eyed fascination. Some of the braver boys and girls challenged the front row with mock charges, only to scurry away when they lifted their sticks.

Petra ignored the children for a moment and studied the sea of masks, all of them identical, all of them fierce. Only one protestor was unmasked, the young woman they called Viola. Petra watched as she took a step forwards, clasped her hands in front of her, and prepared to speak. That was when Petra noticed the drones, flitting into position to cover all the angles; they began broadcasting to the DataStream the moment Viola stepped forwards.

"I honestly don't know what to do, ma'am," Atii said as she joined Petra by the side of the SUV, she acknowledged Seabloom with a brief nod. She switched to English for his benefit. "I thought about forming a line as we did at the bridge, but we haven't got the numbers to resist."

"And even if I emptied the base," Seabloom said, "I'm not sure it would make much difference. Do you have water cannons?"

Petra almost laughed. "No," she said. "And we don't want to turn the street into an ice rink."

"No," he said. "I didn't think of that."

"Tear gas is out, too," Atii said. "We've just never had to deal with a demonstration on this scale." She shook her head. "I don't like it."

"I think," Petra said, "the decision has been made for us. We will just have to hear what she wants to say and take it from there. However…" She scanned the ranks of police officers and vehicles assembled in a hatched formation across the street. "I suggest equipping all officers with riot shields and body armour. Just do it quietly, Atii. I don't want to force their hand."

Atii nodded and jogged around the car to give the order. Petra watched as the Sergeants dispersed to organise the remaining officers. Seabloom stamped his feet as he watched the line. He grinned at Petra and she saw tiny beads of frost pearl around the hairs above his lip. There was a hush, and then Viola began to speak.

"I speak for the dispossessed," she said, her voice amplified by the drone hovering directly above her. "Those too old to be cared for, and too young to be heard. We are the middle generation of students and apprentices, the untrained and uneducated, the poorly paid, the homeless and the unemployed. We are

Greenlanders, all of us, though we have no common tongue. We are Greenlanders, all, though we do not look the same, act the same, nor live the same way as our ancestors, not even our parents and grandparents. We are the post-colonials, the refuse and the unwanted, but we are the future. Ignore us at your peril, for we are not placid or weak. Our parents and grandparents agreed to laws that will outlive them and poison our future. They supported outdated ideas and older referendums when we were too young to vote, and they voted with their hearts, when they should have voted with their heads. Our heads may be young, but our minds are bright, and our hearts big enough to embrace the whole of Greenland, its mountains, the ice, glaciers, the rocks, the birds, beasts, the men, women and children of Greenland, now and in the future, ours, and theirs. But we will not be unheard, we will not be unseen, and we will not be idle." The rows of young men and women bristled, and their masks steamed with appreciative comments and enthusiastic laughs together with the turning and nodding of heads. Viola continued, "January 6th is the Epiphany, the manifestation of Christ. But it is also the day of *mitaartut* when we embrace our Greenlandic traditions and call upon our friends and our family to recognise us, challenging them to call us by our true names, no matter the disguise, the masks, or the paint. Today," she said, "we have had our epiphany, we have come to that great realisation that the future is ours, that we have more at stake than ever before, and that we will have our say, we will be heard." Viola paused as the young Greenlanders roared and shrieked. "We will decide our future, for us, for them," she said and pointed at the children, "and for you. Gone is the day of corrupt governments and hushed deals. Gone too is the day of the colonial power, the casual oppressors." She raised her fist, and said, "On this day, our *mitaartut*, we will call on you and you will recognise us. We will be recognised."

The front row took a step forward.

"We will be seen."

They raised the sticks in their hands.

"We will be heard."

Viola shuffled forwards as the front row parted to each side of her. Petra glanced at Atii and the police formed a line, two ranks deep. Gloved hands flexed around shields. Visors were pulled down to cover the officers' faces as the protestors took another step forward. Viola joined them.

"We will not be forgotten…"

Viola paused as a police officer, a woman, broke through the ranks of police shields. The officer stepped in front of Viola and placed her hand on the pistol holstered at her waist. Two drones flew in on either side of Viola, the dull light of day reflected in the large round camera lenses as the police officer drew her sidearm.

"Atii," Petra shouted, pointing at the police officer aiming her pistol at Viola's face. "Stop her."

Viola's eyes widened as she stared through the visor obscuring the police officer's face. The creases of fear on Viola's forehead softened as she recognised the face behind the gun. Atii burst through the police line as the officer held her pistol in a two-handed grip and fired.

"No," Petra shouted.

She took a step forward. Seabloom grabbed her

arm and she jerked it free, stumbling towards the protestors as Viola slumped to the ground. Her blood pooled beneath her head, spreading across the smooth snow covering the road. The officer fired three more shots into the air above the crowd and the protestors scattered for a second, long enough for her to turn and kick Atii to the ground, before darting across the street, and disappearing between two patrol cars blocking a side street.

The protestors rallied, surging towards Atii as she scrambled to her feet. The police rushed forwards to meet them, locking their shields together to protect their Sergeant from an onslaught of sticks, boots and venom.

"Wait, Petra," Seabloom said. He reached for her again, but again she pulled free of his grasp.

Petra twisted to see Viola's body being dragged away from the clash of sticks and riot shields. She turned again to glimpse the back of the police officer running away from the street and picking her way between the rocks towards a long low block of apartments. Petra ran after her.

"Commissioner, wait."

Petra slowed long enough to see a police SUV skid to a stop a few metres to her right. Aron's breath steamed out of the open window as he fumbled with his seatbelt, opened the door and scrambled out of the driver's seat.

"Aron," she shouted, "you're with me."

"Don't be stupid, Petra."

Petra heard Seabloom's voice and ignored him. She focused on the distance between her and the police officer leaping between outcrops of rock poking out of the snow between the houses and apartments. The officer stopped to aim her pistol at the drone following her, disabling it with just a few shots, suggesting an intimacy with the design, and a flair for accuracy. She holstered her pistol and removed her helmet, tossing it to one side as the drone crashed into the side of the Post Office building. The shock of blonde hair surprised Petra, her breath catching in her throat as she recognised Natuk. The rogue officer's face was wet with tears, her lips wrenched with pain, and she glared at Petra for a split-second, before jumping off the rocky outcrop and skidding onto the icy street below. Petra caught her breath and gave chase.

"Ma'am," Aron said as he ran beside her. "Permission to run faster?"

"Granted," Petra said. She cursed her lack of activity during the winter months as Aron peeled away from her and chased Natuk deeper into the residential area. Petra jogged after him, pausing at the side of a building to rest, and then cursing again as she saw Natuk use a frozen drainpipe to climb onto a low asphalt roof, scattering ravens as she climbed onto the next longer roof covering the apartment block. Petra kept running.

"Ma'am."

Petra looked up as Aron reached down from the first low roof to take her hand. Her feet slipped on the drainpipe as she climbed, causing Aron to grunt as he pulled her up. They ran to the next roof together, the ravens cawing and flapping about their heads as Aron laced his fingers into a step for Petra to step onto. He lifted her up and she scrambled onto the roof. Aron joined her a second later and they pounded across the bare bitumen just as Natuk reached the gap between two roofs.

"She'll jump," Aron said, as she slowed to a jog. Petra slowed beside him. "I don't want to force her, ma'am," he said.

"Neither do I," Petra said.

She stopped as Natuk turned and drew her pistol. Aron reached for his, but Petra stopped him with a shake of her head and a cautionary wave of her hand.

"She's armed, ma'am."

"I'm not blind, Aron."

"I know, but…"

"There has to be another way," Petra said.

Natuk shifted her stance and took aim. Petra stopped. She looked at the young police officer, the woman she imagined to be a younger version of herself, so full of energy and opinions. *But I was but a shadow of Natuk*, she thought, as she considered just how determined Natuk was. *Determined enough to kill me*, she realised, *the one who murdered her brother.*

"Can we talk, Natuk?" Petra said. She motioned for Aron to stay on her right.

"I've got nothing to say, *ma'am*."

Her last word surprised Petra. It could be an act, some kind of diversion. But Petra hoped it was something else, a last vestige of hope, that Natuk – deep down – might still be the exemplary officer that she was, before she was corrupted and poisoned to pursue such a dangerous and tragic path. Petra remembered the photos on the Ombudsman's wall, the ones of Natuk and her twin brother sharing a birthday, several birthdays. She was reminded that the poisoning of Natuk's mind had begun long before she wore the uniform of a police officer, and long before she shot and killed that young woman in the street, only moments ago.

"Help me, Aron," Petra whispered. "Give me something."

Aron scuffed his shoe as he shifted his balance from one foot to the other. He stared at Natuk, and then whispered out of the corner of his mouth. "Today is her birthday," he said. "She's twenty-six."

Twenty-six, Petra thought, *and already she is a murderer and a revolutionary.* Petra pressed her hands to her sides and took a deep breath. *She's also one of mine*, she thought, and took a step forwards.

Chapter 24

Gaba waited until the big Greenlander disappeared below decks, pushing the smaller, frailer figure of Ombudsman Anna Riis in front of him. Gaba could have walked towards the trawler, but he decided that when the Captain noticed him, he would have plenty of time to decide if he should leave the dock and drive out to sea. *No*, Gaba thought, *I may as well run. If nothing else, it might make him panic.* Gaba jogged across the short beach to the rocks beneath the parking area and the old wooden dock. The pounding of his boots on the slippery wooden slats vibrated through the dock and into the hull of the trawler, the Captain looked up just as Gaba gripped the rail and vaulted onto the deck. He slid on the icy surface all the way to the wheelhouse and wrenched the door open.

The Captain grabbed a pistol from a holster glued to the side of a wood panel below the windows of the bridge; he turned and fired, clipping Gaba's shoulder. Gaba cursed as he crossed the short deck to the Captain's chair. He closed his fist around the pistol, pulled it free of the Captain's grip, and slammed it into the man's forehead. The Captain slumped to the deck, as Gaba held the pistol in front of him on his way to the stairs leading below decks.

A short burst of bullets ripped through the door at the bottom of the stairs forcing Gaba to take cover behind the nearest bulkhead. He held the pistol in a tight two-handed grip and peered around the bulkhead only to snap his head back at the sight of the Greenlander below decks taking aim. Gaba slid away from the stairs and rolled to the door as a second, longer burst of fire forced him to open the door to the working area of the trawler behind the wheelhouse. Gaba slipped on the rime ice coating the steps and roared as he scraped his shin on the last step. He stumbled across the deck towards the thick plastic fish bins lashed to the trawler's starboard side. The Greenlander shoved the rear door open with the muzzle of a submachine gun – a Heckler and Koch MP5, Gaba's preferred weapon of choice.

Gaba leaned against the fish bin and allowed himself a short chuckle. The last few years running Âmo Security had been dull compared to the last few minutes. He had tried convincing himself that he was a father now, that he was getting too old for this game, but he missed it. He might even admit to being more or less addicted to the thrill of action. Atii knew it, and she told him about it at every opportunity.

"One day it will get the better of you," she had said, "and where will that leave me and the boys?"

She was right, Gaba just hadn't realised that day had come. He listened for the Greenlander's footsteps, some indication that he was moving across the deck. But it was quiet, apart from the distant sounds of cheering, or shouting, coming from the city centre.

He's waiting, Gaba thought. *Clever man.*

"That's what I'd do," Gaba called out. "Find a good position and wait."

"What do you know about it?" the Greenlander said.

Gaba turned his head slightly and imagined the man to be hiding in cover on the port side of the trawler, somewhere beneath the wheelhouse.

"I used to do this for a living," Gaba said.

"And now?"

"Now?" Gaba laughed. "More of a hobby really."

"Dangerous hobby."

"Tell me about it. My wife wants me to quit." Gaba waited for the man to speak, or move, perhaps both. When nothing happened, he tried again. "My name's Gaba Alatak."

"Angut."

"Just Angut?"

"Samuelsen."

Gaba checked the magazine in the pistol. The weight of it suggested it was half full, with another round in the chamber. About six shots, if he was being generous. More likely there were just five.

Not enough.

"Samuelsen? You related to Sammy Samuelsen?"

"*Naamik.*"

"No? How about Jens Jensen?"

Gaba flicked his head at the sound of movement, footsteps, a slow, almost silent shuffle across the deck.

"You're starting to annoy me," Angut said.

His voice was closer, as if he had crossed the deck. Gaba stuck the barrel of the pistol over the lip of the bin and fired a snapshot before rolling to his left. Gaba fired again, clipping Angut's knee. Gaba's third shot caught him in the shin and the fourth in his thigh as he worked his way up the man's body. Gaba aimed at Angut's chest as the Greenlander raised the MP5. The pistol was lighter in Gaba's hand, he should have known that all his bullets were spent, but he pulled the trigger anyway, and then launched himself at Angut as the MP5 stuttered another three-round burst. The bark was worse than the bite as the cold air seemed to press the rapid crack of the submachine gun down upon the deck, the weapons fire echoed around the sides of the trawler as Gaba landed on Angut's body and slammed his fist into the Greenlander's knee. He reached for the MP5 but received an elbow in his face instead. Gaba spluttered a gob full of blood from his mouth and scrabbled across the slippery deck as Angut cursed his mangled leg, reached for the railings and pulled himself to his feet. He kicked Gaba in the head as he crawled towards him.

"I've heard of you," Angut said, as he aimed a second kick at Gaba, catching the retired SRU Sergeant in the jaw. "You're the dog that killed Ooqi."

Gaba rolled out of Angut's reach, scrabbling to his feet as Angut pulled himself along the railings towards the rear door of the wheelhouse. Gaba wondered why he didn't fire. He saw Angut wince as he reached for a spare magazine in the cargo pocket of his trousers. Gaba wiped the blood from his face with the back of his hand and launched himself at Angut, slamming him into the railing. The magazine splashed into the water. Gaba ignored Angut's blows to his head and grabbed Angut's good leg, the one without the bullet holes and blood. He lifted it as Angut shifted his grip on the railing and used his elbow to beat down on Gaba's neck. Gaba roared as he lifted Angut up and over the side of the railing. He kicked at Angut's bloody shin, and again as Angut faltered. Gaba twisted and shoved Angut over the side. The big Greenlander slammed into the side of the trawler, gripping the railing with one hand, reaching with the other.

"I was wrong," Gaba said, as he grabbed the MP5

by the sling and pulled it over Angut's head. "I never heard of you." He held the submachine gun by the barrel and slammed the butt into Angut's fingers. "I don't know you." He hit Angut's fingers a second time. "And I don't need to know you, either." Angut spat as he slid down the side of the trawler. The splash he made in the water sent a small wave that rippled into the smooth chunks of ice bobbing by the side of the boat. Gaba lowered the MP5 and waited for Angut to slip beneath the surface. "It *is* a dangerous hobby," he said, as he gritted his teeth and walked to the wheelhouse door.

Gaba tossed the submachine gun onto a bench just inside the door. He checked the wound on his arm, explored his jaw and nose with tentative fingers, stopping when he heard the bone in his nose crackle. He wiped the blood on his trousers and shuffled to the top of the stairs, tilting his head at the sound of raised voices and a single shot. There was another shot and more voices, identical to the first, almost as if they were looped. Gaba climbed down the stairs and pushed at the door into the living area below decks.

Anna Riis was thinner than Gaba remembered. The last time he had seen her, she was entertaining the Dutch Jonkheer in her cosy wooden residence close to the water. She was even closer to the water now, but there was nothing cosy about her surroundings. Anna Riis' legs were sprawled on the floor at odd angles, as if she had been shoved and did not have the strength to stand. She leaned against the side of the bench seat beside the table and watched a video sequence looping on the media screen mounted to the bulkhead. Gaba heard the shot, saw the close-up of the police officer, a woman in full riot gear, her pistol extended in front of her in a two-handed grip. The camera switched to a different angle catching a young woman's fall as the bullet from the police officer's gun punctured her skull and removed the better part of the back of her head. Gaba saw the mess on the snow beneath the young woman's head, recognised it for what it was, and then stared at the screen as the camera switched to a third angle, showing the police rushing forwards to protect an officer on the ground.

"Atii," he said, and took a step towards the screen.

"It's alright," Anna said. "They save her. Although the police take a beating. You'll see it in the next sequence, after another close-up of the girl." She turned her head to look at Gaba. "They call her Viola. She's a martyr now. Greenland's first."

Anna took Gaba's hand when he offered it to her. She pushed down on the seat as he pulled her up. Anna perched at the edge of the seat, her back to the media screen, as Gaba slumped onto the bench opposite her.

"Is he dead?" she asked. "Angut?"

Gaba nodded.

"And the Captain."

Gaba cursed as he realised he had forgotten all about the Captain.

"Not dead. Knocked out, maybe."

Anna shrugged. "It doesn't matter anymore. It's all over." She glanced at the screen before looking at Gaba. "She was supposed to turn the people against the government, to make them question the First Minister, to sour and stall the move to independence." Anna shook her head. "Anarchy wasn't part of the plan. I underestimated her."

"Who?"

"Natuk. My foster daughter."

"You think she wants to turn Greenland on itself?"

"What do *you* think she's done, Sergeant?"

"I'm not a police officer."

"Not anymore, maybe, but you know how this looks. She has made a martyr and turned the youth of Greenland against the very institution that remains fully Danish – the police and the justice system. They will tear this country apart."

"You don't know that."

"Hah, forgive me," Anna said, "I forgot for a moment who I was talking to. You're the Commissioner's pit bull. The one that killed my boy."

"It's funny," Gaba said. He pointed at the image of Natuk pointing and firing her pistol as it flashed onto the screen. "You call her your *foster* daughter, but Ooqi Kleemann is your boy. I might not mix in the same social circles as you and your Danish cronies, but even I can imagine how a good dollop of favouritism might split a family, and turn a daughter against her own mother, foster or not."

Gaba stood up. He pulled a winter jacket from a hook behind the door and tossed it at the Ombudsman.

"Put it on," he said.

"Are we going somewhere?"

Gaba pointed at the screen. "We're going into the city. We're going to stop this."

"Really, Sergeant. And how do you imagine we're going to do that?"

"Oh, I don't know. You're the clever, devious, one. I'm sure you'll figure something out."

Gaba waited for Anna to pull on the jacket and then pushed her towards the stairs. The Captain groaned as Gaba searched his pockets. He tugged a pair of car keys out of the man's shirt pocket and slapped him on the cheek. Gaba pulled the keys for the boat out of the ignition and stuffed them into his pocket.

"Don't leave town, Captain," he said, as he gripped Anna by the arm and guided her to the wheelhouse door.

"You really think I can stop this?" Anna laughed, as she slid across the icy deck. "You're mad."

"That's right," Gaba said. "It's Petra that is the brains in this partnership. Don't underestimate her, like you did your daughter." Gaba helped the Ombudsman onto the dock and clicked the Captain's car keys. The lights of a small electric town car flashed and Gaba sighed, thankful that he didn't have to walk back to his own car, thankful for the small things. Petra would have to deal with the bigger things, like saving the country.

Chapter 25

The distance between Petra and Natuk could be measured in ravens. The wingtip scratches in the snow shadowed from the sun stretched between them, perhaps three ravens, or one flapping and hopping over the other. Petra could hear them scratching across the roof, their claws biting into the bitumen as they stalked and hopped their way towards the three police officers staring at one another at the edge of the roof, the ravens' domain. They weren't alone; a drone hovered nearby, darting backwards and forwards and then holding its position, as if uncertain as to how to proceed. Natuk waved her pistol at Petra, forcing her to stop as she put on a pair of thick-rimmed glasses. Her left eye flickered back and forth while her right focused on Petra. The drone retreated and Natuk slipped the glasses into her pocket.

"It's the cold," she said. "I have to keep them warm."

Petra nodded, as if it was perfectly normal to discuss practical matters during a standoff that was Mexican by nature, and yet typically Greenlandic; the ravens seemed happy to perform the role of desert vultures, and Petra knew Aron had his hand curled around the grip of his police issue pistol. A thin sheet of snow curled across the roof, dusting their boots as Natuk shifted her grip on her pistol.

"I've been here before, Natuk," Petra said. "Two weeks ago."

"Don't," Natuk said. Her aim wavered as she shook her head. "Don't tell me about my brother."

"It was like this." Petra gestured at Aron behind

her with a subtle wave of her hand. "Three of us. It didn't have to end in his death." Petra took a breath and a tiny step towards Natuk.

"I saw what happened." Natuk swallowed. She flexed her fingers around the grip of her pistol.

"Yes, but do you know why he reached for his gun?"

"I know why. It was for the cause. He did it for our foster mother. She put him there," Natuk said. She raised the gun, changing her aim from Petra's chest to her head. "But you killed him."

"I don't agree," Petra said. "I know I killed him, I have to live with that, but that's not why he died, why he chose to die. He was sending a message, Natuk. He put his glasses on the table so that you could see what happened. That message, tragic and brutal – it was for his sister. It was for you."

Natuk laughed. "You think so? Alright, *ma'am*. What was he trying to tell me? What was the message?"

"I think it was a warning," Petra said. "I think he was trying to tell you not to follow him. He wanted you to know the consequences of listening to your foster mother, to show you how she had poisoned him, so that he could save you." Petra took another step forward. "He loved you, Natuk."

Natuk lowered the pistol and glanced over her shoulder. She shuffled closer to the edge of the roof. The boldest of the three ravens stalked closer, tapping its claws on the metal gutter as it stared at Natuk.

"He always was the more emotional one." Natuk looked at the gap between the roofs, judging the distance.

"Was he older than you?"

"What?"

"You were twins. Was he born first?"

"We never knew," Natuk said. "Our parents never told us. But I think I was the firstborn. I was oldest."

"He would have been twenty-six today," Petra said. "Just like you."

"Hey," Natuk said. She raised her arm as she leaned to one side, pointing her pistol at Aron as he inched closer to Petra. "Stop there, Aron."

"He's your friend, Natuk."

"I don't have *friends*," she said. "I use people, until they are no longer useful."

"Like Tiina Markussen?"

"What?" Natuk's eyes narrowed as she switched her gaze and the pistol from Aron back to Petra.

"You called her Viola. But her name was Tiina."

"I know what her name was."

"Was she not a friend, or was she just *useful?*"

"Tiina was a friend. I liked her," Natuk said. The pistol wavered as she took a breath. "But Viola is very useful."

"*Is?*"

Natuk nodded towards the main street running through the city, just behind Petra. The cool air rumbled with protest. "What do you think?"

"I can see that," Petra said. "But what now? You've created a martyr and sowed the seeds of anarchy. What's next?"

"I don't need a next," Natuk said. She turned her head slightly, flicking her gaze from the edge to the roof opposite. "I'm just looking for a way out."

"You mean you're done? You're finished?" It was Petra's turn to laugh. "Not only have you killed a friend, Natuk, you've dishonoured your brother. He might have been misguided, but he wasn't a coward…"

"Ma'am," Aron said, his words soft, closer than Petra anticipated. "Be careful."

"You're calling *me* a coward?"

"Because you've given up on Greenland," Petra said. "If you truly loved your country, and if you believed in what your brother was doing, then you wouldn't stop now, now that there is so much work to be done."

"You understand *nothing*," Natuk said. Spittle flew from her mouth and the pistol shook in her hand. "What have *you* done for your country? When did you stand up for something? I don't remember hearing you challenge the First Minister when she signed the deal with the Chinese, or again, when my so-called foster mother brokered another shitty deal with the Dutch. Where were you? What would Maratse think of you?"

Petra shuddered for a second as Natuk hurled David's name at her.

"That's what I thought," Natuk said. "You're ashamed. You never spoke up." She laughed. "I heard a rumour once that you never voted. That the referendum was your first time. Imagine that, a Police Commissioner that doesn't vote."

"It's not my place to…"

"Not your place? It's *exactly* your place – as a Greenlander, you have to vote. You can't sit on the fence, you have to be active, to take a stand, like them," she said, and pointed the pistol towards the protestors clashing with the police less than half a kilometre away. "But no, you waited to cast the first real vote of your professional life when Greenland was weakest, when the whole country voted with their heart, not their heads. Someone should have used their head. Someone should have challenged the government, forced them to clean up their act before committing to a future that will have us on our knees before we reach the end of our first year of independence."

"That's what you think?"

"It's what I *know*," Natuk said. "It's what you know too."

"You call me a coward, but you could have done something about it."

"I did." Natuk jabbed the muzzle of the pistol towards the city.

"From behind a mask, Natuk. It's not the same."

"Sometimes you need to use a mask to send a message. One face can make a difference. I gave them two. I gave Greenland the mask for the people, and Viola's face – her memory – to lead them. I've played my part. I just need to exit now."

"This is not a play, Natuk."

"You're wrong, ma'am." Natuk spread her arms like raven wings. "*All the world's a stage,*" she said. "*And all the men and women merely players; They have their exits and their entrances…*" She bowed once, turning the gun back towards Petra as she applied pressure to the trigger. "This is my exit," she said. "And yours."

Petra heard Aron's boots scrape across the roof as Natuk squeezed the trigger. She felt his hand on her shoulder as he shoved her to the ground, and she heard the *whoomph* of the air escaping from his lungs as Natuk's bullet punched into his chest. He had never been a frontline officer, he never wore body armour, and he never fully understood, like Petra did, that his devotion to duty might one day get him killed. Aron's body crumpled onto the roof and his pistol skittered onto a patch of wind-blown snow as Petra slid onto her side. She saw Natuk run towards her, and then watched her turn, tossing her pistol to one side as she ran for the edge of the roof, arms pumping. Natuk leaped, slamming into the roof opposite, the toes of her boots scraping against the building's wooden façade as she gripped the gutter and clawed her way onto the roof.

Natuk rolled onto her side and rested for a second. Her chest heaved, and she pressed her hand to her ribs, grimacing as she probed the part of her body that had been the first to strike the side of the building. She didn't see or hear Petra pick up Aron's pistol, and the first bullet flipped her onto her back as she tried to stand.

"Stay down, Natuk," Petra shouted. "Just stay down."

Petra kicked at the snow on the roof. She kicked at the ravens, cursing them as they flapped out of reach, taunting her just like their cousins had taunted Maratse's dogs further north, in Inussuk, where she should be, where they should have stayed. It was Petra who had pushed for them to move back to the city. It was Petra who had accepted the job as Commissioner.

"And I'm the one responsible for the dead," she said, pressing the grip of the gun to the side of her head as blinked away the tears cooling on her eyelashes to look at Aron's body.

You're not responsible, Piitalaat.

"Yes, David, I am."

Eeqqi. You're not.

Petra palmed the tears from her eyes and took a deep breath of cool air.

"You don't understand, David. I *am* responsible. These are *my* officers." She looked across the gap between the roofs and watched as Natuk pressed a hand to her bloody shoulder and tried to stand. "All of them."

David's voice retreated to the last quiet place in her mind. She imagined he was brooding, although he never brooded. He would just observe, quietly, biding his time, until it was time to act. She bit back another tear and smiled at the thought. People always underestimated Constable David Maratse. That's what she loved about him. That and many other things.

It's time to act, Piitalaat.

"I know," she said.

Just be careful.

"I will," she said, as she took three steps back, stuffed the pistol into her pocket and ran towards the edge of the roof.

Petra's fingers slapped against the side of the gutter on the opposite roof with a dull thud. She grasped the gutter with just three fingers of her left hand as gravity tugged at her body, her legs flailing as the ravens flapped and cawed in the gap between the roofs. The pistol slipped out of her pocket as Petra twisted. She cried out as she felt her fingers slip and the metal gutter begin to bend. She looked down, saw the snow plume where the pistol fell, and imagined landing on top of it, her back broken by the fall and Greenland in pieces.

She felt cold fingers wrap around her wrist, and a fierce energy that trembled into her arm. Petra lifted her head and looked into Natuk's eyes as the rogue police officer leaned over the edge of the roof.

"You have to reach up with your other hand," she said. "I can only use one arm. You shot the other."

Petra raised her right hand, stretching her fingers until she felt the cold bite of metal and gripped it. She scraped her boots against the wall as Natuk pulled her up until Petra could hook her elbow over the edge. Natuk shifted her grip, grabbing Petra's belt as she shifted her position to kneel on the roof and drag Petra's body up and over the gutter.

"You're too old to jump, ma'am," Natuk said, as she clawed Petra onto her lap.

"I know," Petra said, as she caught her breath. She looked at Natuk. "You could have let me fall. Why didn't you?"

"Aron," she said, with a nod towards the opposite roof. "He was Ooqi's friend. He was kind to him, to both of us. He was never meant to die." Natuk wiped a bloody hand over her face, hiding the tears welling in her eyes. "I don't know what to do next. I don't know where to go, or what to do when I get there."

Petra sat on the roof and pulled Natuk into her body. She wrapped her arms around her, brushed the grit and snow from Natuk's short blonde hair and held her as she sobbed. Petra stared at Aron's body, and then shifted her gaze to the city and the clash of police and protestors – the clash of *Greenlanders*, fighting for their future and the survival of their country. Petra looked at the rough bands of ink tattooed into the joints between her fingers.

I know all about survival, she thought. *And now it's*

time to act. To make a difference. To fight for Greenland's future.

Chapter 26

The Fire Chief beckoned for Petra to join him beside the fire engine as two voluntary firefighters strapped Aron's body onto a spinal board and prepared to move him to the ground.

"You never checked his body, did you?" the Fire Chief asked, when Petra joined him.

"No," she said. "I jumped off the roof just a few minutes after he was shot."

"You jumped off the roof…" the Chief laughed. "Well, if you'd *stayed* on the roof, you might have noticed he was breathing." He pointed at the ambulance where the paramedics wrapped a dressing around Natuk's shoulder. "She didn't kill him." He pointed at the firefighters passing Aron over the railings of the bucket lift. "He's unconscious, but he will recover. They're expecting him at Kong Frederik's."

"That's good," Petra said. Her shoulders sagged as she smiled.

"What about you, Commissioner, you look tired. Are you hurt?"

"I don't have time to be tired or hurt, Chief." Petra nodded towards a thin twist of smoke rising above Nuuk's main street. "I've got to sort this mess out."

"It is a mess," he said. "Honestly, I don't know what they're all fighting over. We all want the same thing. Don't we?"

"What *do* we want?" Petra pressed her hand on the Chief's bulky sleeve and smiled. "Look after Aron for me." She took a last look at the firefighters in the bucket lift, and then beckoned to the officer guarding

Natuk. "What's the situation on *Aqqusinersuaq*?"

"Ugly," he said, and then, "lots of shouting. The smoke is from a burning car – one of ours."

"Any casualties?"

"Lots of bruises. Sergeant Napa has a concussion but try telling her that."

Petra smiled at the thought of Atii brushing off any concerns for her health as she cursed and coordinated her colleagues into order.

"I can imagine. What about the protestors?"

"They are mad as hell, and they just got madder when the Americans arrived. They've moved back down the street, but they are rallying. Atii… Sergeant Napa thinks they are going to charge again. She's not sure they can stop them a second time."

Petra struggled to imagine a charge. She thought the disturbance would be more sporadic, with a constant push backwards and forwards between small groups probing the police lines. But so long as their aggression was directed at the police, Petra thought there was a chance to keep innocent bystanders out of harm's way.

But we're all in this together, she thought, as she walked with the officer to the back of the ambulance.

"Are you ready, Natuk?" she asked.

"I thought I was taking her into custody," the officer said.

"Not yet." Petra held out her hand to steady Natuk as she stepped out of the ambulance. "We've got work to do."

The officer drove them to the end of the side street, parking as close to the police lines as possible. He held the door for Petra as she got out of the car. He fumbled with the cuffs on his belt and gestured towards Natuk, but Petra shook her head.

"You've got her gun," she said. "And she won't run. Not this time."

Natuk nodded and followed Petra to the back of the police lines.

"Have you still got control of the drones?" Petra asked.

"If you let me put my glasses on."

"I want you to film this, so, yes, put your glasses on and have two drones follow us."

"Where are we going?"

"To talk to them," Petra said. She pointed at the line of protestors.

Atii stepped away from the police line as soon as she saw Petra. She stopped beside a body lying on the ground between two police patrol vehicles. The corner of the thin sheet covering it snapped gently in the wind, and Natuk stared at it. Strands of Viola's hair were just visible clinging to the edge of the sheet. Petra took Natuk's arm and held her gently as Atii approached.

"I heard you found her," Atii said. Her lip curled slightly as she looked at Natuk. "I heard she shot Aron."

"He needs help, but he's going to be okay."

"What are we going to do with her?"

"I honestly don't know," Petra said. "We're going to go down there and see what happens."

"I don't think that's a good idea, ma'am," Atii said. "And I'm pretty sure Seabloom will agree with me."

"Where is he?"

"On the right side of the street. He has two groups of Seamen like wedges on each side. They're armed, and they're aggressive. I don't like it, but the protestors have backed off."

"Greenlanders," Petra said. "We have to look beyond the masks, Atii."

Atii started to speak but the words hung in her mouth as she looked around Petra at the car approaching the rear of the police lines. Gaba grinned from behind the wheel. He was still grinning as he opened the door and got out of the car.

"What happened to you?" Atii said. "And why are you bleeding?"

"I'm still bleeding?"

Gaba opened the passenger door and helped Anna Riis out of the car. She tensed at the sight of Natuk, and Gaba gripped her arm.

"I guess this is a family reunion," he said, and grinned at Petra. "Told you I'd find her."

"Yes, you did," she said.

Natuk bent down as if to tie the laces of her boots. She lifted the cuff of her trouser leg and pulled the compact pistol from her ankle holster. Atii reached for her sidearm as Natuk pointed her backup pistol at her foster mother.

"Stand down, Natuk," Petra said, as she stepped between them, cursing herself for not having searched her for hidden weapons.

"Step aside, ma'am," Natuk said.

Petra shook her head, waving a discreet hand at Atii as the SRU Sergeant started to move around Natuk's flank.

"I will shoot you if you get in my way," Natuk said.

"Killing her won't help," Petra said. She pointed towards the young Greenlanders regrouping further down the street. "They need to hear what she has to say. They need to know what she has done. If you kill her, there's no turning back. Greenland will be lost. There will be no future, only pain." Petra walked towards Natuk. "There's been enough pain, already. Don't you think, Natuk?"

Petra heard heavy feet sliding and scuffing across the snow and imagined Gaba moving in front of Anna Riis, shielding her from Natuk. The look on Atii's face confirmed it.

"I should have killed her on the boat," Natuk said, as she lowered the pistol. She dropped the pistol onto the ground. The wind flapped at the sheet, and the corner lifted to reveal Viola's face and the neat black hole in her forehead. Her eyes were open, frozen wide in disbelief.

Atii covered Petra as she stooped to pick up the pistol. Petra handed it to Atii and then turned to look at the Ombudsman.

"It's time to tell the people what you have done," she said. "It's time to stop this, to put an end to your machinations."

"Machinations?" Anna laughed. "That's a fine word coming from you, *Commissioner.*"

Petra nodded. She picked at a spot of blood on her fingers, studied the bands between the joints. "That's what you think, isn't it? That we're all simple. That Greenland can't survive without the help of another, more sophisticated people watching over them." The winter sun broke through the clouds and the corners of Petra's mouth curled as if they were attached to the sun's rays like strings. She smiled, stuffing her hands into her pockets, just as she had seen Maratse do so many times when they were out on the ice, or even when walking through the city. *My city*, she thought.

"My dear Commissioner," Anna said. "Is this going to be your moment, your speech, when you tell me just how strong and independent Greenlanders can be, how they must be allowed to make their own mistakes? It's all very touching, and boring. I've heard it before. Too many times. The people I represent…"

"Are standing right over there," Petra said. "You were employed as Ombudsman in Greenland. You were the supposed to be the voice of the people. If they had concerns or grievances regarding the government, it was you they were meant to come to. You were the people's advocate, and you failed. You are not the check and balance. You were not supposed to play God or take on the role of a secret dictator. You were supposed to listen and serve."

Petra paused at the sight of a government car approaching from the hotel at the bottom of the hill. It stopped just behind the Ombudsman, and Greenland's First Minister stepped out. Petra gestured for Natuk to put on her glasses and looked up as a ring of drones moved into position above them.

"The people are listening," Petra said. "It's time for you to serve."

"It's cold, Commissioner," Anna said. She shivered for effect. "Perhaps if we did this inside?"

Petra turned at the sound of boots padding, sliding and scuffing on the snow as the young people of Greenland filled the spaces between the police and their patrol cars. They removed their masks and dropped their sticks as the police lifted their visors and lowered their shields.

"This is interesting, Petra," Seabloom said, as he

pushed through the crowd to stand beside her. "It's also potentially dangerous." He lowered his voice. "I can get you out, but it has to be now."

"No," she said. "I want to hear what she has to say."

"I don't think she's going to say anything at all."

"She will," Petra said. "We're not leaving until she does."

Gaba let go of Anna's arm and stepped to one side. He walked over to a police car and leaned against it, grimacing as he moved his leg until it was comfortable. He smiled at Petra and took Atii's hand as she joined him.

"You're in trouble," she said.

"I usually am," he said.

"But you enjoyed yourself, didn't you?"

"More than you want to know."

Gaba stopped talking as the First Minister stepped into a gap as two of the protestors made room for her in a tight circle around the Ombudsman. The drones pulled back as Natuk positioned them, dragging, dropping, and blinking icons in her lenses as she broadcast the drone feed into the DataStream.

"You are under arrest, and you will answer for Tiina's murder…"

"I understand."

"But I want you to record this moment. Make sure that Greenland gets the whole story, and that they understand what has happened here, and why." Petra took Natuk's hand. "I can't and won't pretend that you haven't done the things you have done, Natuk, but neither can I ignore your intelligence and your passion, albeit misguided. You will be punished.

You will be imprisoned, but you are going to serve your country one way or another. You owe Greenland that much."

"And what about you, ma'am?" Natuk asked.

What about me? Petra mused.

She looked at Anna Riis, shivering inside a ring of Greenlanders, the future of the country. She looked at the First Minister, at Gaba and Atii, and she looked at the faces of the young men and women, the children squeezing between their legs, and the older generations gathering behind them. A future Greenland, independent of Denmark, free to make its own mistakes, and create its own opportunities, would need its own police force, to serve the people, and lend a helping hand where needed, to do the heavy lifting when required.

"What about me?" Petra said.

Natuk let go of Petra's hand as a small girl pushed through the ring of people and walked right up to Petra. Quaa grinned as Petra lifted her into her arms.

"I thought you were on your way to Denmark?" Petra said. She smiled at Iiluuna standing on the opposite side of the circle.

Quaa shook her head. "The doctor came back to work today. We're staying in Nuuk," she said.

Petra pulled her close and kissed her forehead. "What a coincidence. So am I."

Snow drifted through the sun's rays, glistening as it fell, dusting the crowd's heads and shoulders. Petra wondered at Anna Riis' stubborn streak, and how long it would take before she cracked. The look on Pipaluk's face suggested she was thinking the same thing. They were not alone.

"I'm curious, Petra," Seabloom said. "Just how long is this going to take?"

Petra shrugged. "As long as necessary," she said. "We're a patient people. We're not going anywhere."

The thought of sticking around and doing her job just a little longer brought a smile to Petra's lips. She felt a sense of peace settle in her mind, like a thick blanket she could curl up in. She closed her eyes for a moment, searching the darkness until she saw his image and heard his voice.

That's good, Piitalaat. I'm happy for you.

Petra clung to Maratse's last words for as long as she could, sad at the thought that they were his last, but happy that he was ready to leave her, happy that they both might find peace. When the Ombudsman finally opened her mouth to speak, Petra smiled at the thought that Greenland might now be able to settle, and that a new sense of peace and understanding would allow them to face whatever challenges lay ahead. For one thing was certain, there would be plenty of them.

The End

About the Author

Christoffer Petersen is the author's pen name. He lives in Denmark. Chris started writing stories about Greenland while teaching in Qaanaaq, the largest village in the very north of Greenland – the population peaked at 600 during the two years he lived there. Chris spent a total of seven years in Greenland, teaching in remote communities and at the Police Academy in the capital of Nuuk.

Chris continues to be inspired by the vast icy wilderness of the Arctic and his books have a common setting in the region, with a Scandinavian influence. He has also watched enough Bourne movies to no longer be surprised by the plot, but not enough to get bored.

You can find Chris in Denmark or online here:

www.christoffer-petersen.com

By the same author:

THE GREENLAND CRIME SERIES
featuring Constable David Maratse

Book 1
SEVEN GRAVES, ONE WINTER

Book 2
BLOOD FLOE

Book 3
WE SHALL BE MONSTERS

Short stories from the same series
KATABATIC
CONTAINER
TUPILAQ
THE LAST FLIGHT
THE HEART THAT WAS A WILD GARDEN

and

THE GREENLAND TRILOGY
featuring Konstabel Fenna Brongaard

Book 1
THE ICE STAR

Book 2
IN THE SHADOW OF THE MOUNTAIN

Book 3
THE SHAMAN'S HOUSE

Printed in Great Britain
by Amazon